The Most Interesting People in Politics: 250 Anecdotes

David Bruce

Published by David Bruce, 2023.

While every precaution has been taken in the preparation of this book, the publisher assumes no responsibility for errors or omissions, or for damages resulting from the use of the information contained herein.

THE MOST INTERESTING PEOPLE IN POLITICS: 250 ANECDOTES

First edition. July 20, 2023.

Copyright © 2023 David Bruce.

ISBN: 979-8223945321

Written by David Bruce.

Table of Contents

Dedication

Dedicated to Carl Eugene Bruce and Josephine Saturday Bruce

My father, Carl Eugene Bruce, died on 24 October 2013. He used to work for Ohio Power, and at one time, his job was to shut off the electricity of people who had not paid their bills. He sometimes would find a home with an impoverished mother and some children. Instead of shutting off their electricity, he would tell the mother that she needed to pay her bill or soon her electricity would be shut off. He would write on a form that no one was home when he stopped by because if no one was home he did not have to shut off their electricity.

The best good deed that anyone ever did for my father occurred after a storm that knocked down many power lines. He and other linemen worked long hours and got wet and cold. Their feet were freezing because water got into their boots and soaked their socks. Fortunately, a kind woman gave my father and the other linemen dry socks to wear.

My mother, Josephine Saturday Bruce, died on 14 June 2003. She used to work at a store that sold clothing. One day, an impoverished mother with a baby clothed in rags walked into the store and started shoplifting in an interesting way: The mother took the rags off her baby and dressed the infant in new clothing. My mother knew that this mother could not afford to buy the clothing, but she helped the mother dress her baby and then she watched as the mother walked out of the store without paying.

***

The doing of good deeds is important. As a free person, you can choose to live your life as a good person or as a bad person. To be a good person, do good deeds. To be a bad person, do bad deeds. If you do good deeds, you will become good. If you do bad deeds, you will become bad. To become the person you want to be, act as if you already are that kind of person. Each of us chooses what kind of person we will become. To become a good person, do the things a good person does. To become a bad person, do the things a bad person does. The opportunity to take action to become the kind of person you want to be is yours.

Human beings have free will. According to the Babylonian Niddah 16b, whenever a baby is to be conceived, the Lailah (angel in charge of contraception) takes the drop of semen that will result in the conception and asks God, "Sovereign of the Universe, what is going to be the fate of this drop? Will it develop into a robust or into a weak person? An intelligent or a stupid person? A wealthy or a poor person?" The Lailah asks all these questions, but it does not ask, "Will it develop into a righteous or a wicked person?" The answer to that question lies in the decisions to be freely made by the human being that is the result of the conception.

A Buddhist monk visiting a class wrote this on the chalkboard: "EVERYONE WANTS TO SAVE THE WORLD, BUT NO ONE WANTS TO HELP MOM DO THE DISHES." The students laughed, but the monk then said, "Statistically, it's highly unlikely that any of you will ever have the opportunity to run into a burning orphanage and rescue an infant. But, in the smallest gesture of kindness — a warm smile, holding the door for the person behind you, shoveling the driveway of the elderly person next door — you have committed an act of immeasurable profundity, because to each of us, our life is our universe."

In her book titled *I Have Chosen to Stay and Fight*, comedian Margaret Cho writes, "I believe that we get complimentary snack-size portions of the afterlife, and we all receive them in a different way." For Ms. Cho, many of her snack-size portions of the afterlife come in hip hop music. Other people get different snack-size portions of the afterlife, and we all must be on the lookout for them when they come our way. And perhaps doing good deeds and experiencing good deeds are snack-size portions of the afterlife.

The Zen master Gisan was taking a bath. The water was too hot, so he asked a student to add some cold water to the bath. The student brought a bucket of cold water, added some cold water to the bath, and then threw the rest of the water on a rocky path. Gisan scolded the student: "Everything can be used. Why did you waste the rest of the water by pouring it on the path? There are some plants nearby which could have used the water. What right do you have to waste even a drop of water?" The student became enlightened and changed his name to Tekisui, which means "Drop of Water."

Cover Photograph for *The Most Interesting People in Politics and History: 250 Anecdotes and Stories*

On the Cover: Leonard and Tippie. They are the Manager and Assistant Manager of an Athens, Ohio, singer-songwriter, and they take turns being named employee of the month. They favorite Human is a Woman, and they want you to VOTE FOR WOMEN'S RIGHTS. In case you can't tell them apart, Leonard is next to Tippie.

***

This is a short, quick, and easy read.

Anecdotes are usually short humorous stories. Sometimes they are thought-provoking or informative, not amusing.

***

Educate Yourself
    Read Like A Wolf Eats
    Be Excellent to Each Other
    Books Then, Books Now, Books Forever

***

Do you know a language other than English? If you do, I give you permission to translate this book, copyright your translation, publish or self-publish it, and keep all the royalties for yourself. (Do give me credit, of course, for the original book.)

Chapter 1: From Activism to Crime

Activism

• African-American college students started a unique form of protest in early 1960 when they staged sit-ins. At the time, Jim Crow laws segregating blacks and whites were common in the South. Whites could drink from one drinking fountain, and blacks had to drink from a different drinking fountain. Whites could use one set of restrooms, and blacks had to use a different set of restrooms. This segregation pervaded the South and extended to lunchrooms. To protest the segregation, African-American college students used to go to a whites-only lunchroom, sit down, and wait to be served. They were *not* served; however, they would continue to sit at the lunch counter, taking up a seat that could have been used by a white customer whom the lunchroom would have been happy to serve. Eventually, the lunchrooms began to serve black people.[1]

• When comedian Whoopi Goldberg did a joke about George W. Bush with the word "Bush" having a double meaning, a certain outraged Republican-friendly television network demanded a videotape of Whoopi telling the joke. After hearing this, comedian Kate Clinton says she sent the network a 43-hour videotape of the network's jokes about President Bill Clinton and his little flesh-colored friend. The network returned the videotape. In response to Whoopi's joke, the suits at Slimfast decided to drop her as their spokesperson. Therefore, to show support for Whoopi, Ms. Clinton attempted to organize a protest in which participants would throw Slimfast into the harbor at Provincetown, but the protest fell through. According to Ms. Clinton, the harbormaster wouldn't allow them to throw Slimfast into the water because Slimfast is environmentally toxic.[2]

• TV's Mister Rogers once watched a violent Saturday morning cartoon with a grandson. In the cartoon were lots of machine guns and lots of shooting. Mister Rogers confessed that what he was watching was scary, even to an adult like him. His grandson looked surprised, then said that the bad guys were the people being shot, so Mister Rogers pointed out that there are other and better ways of dealing with bad guys. That night, before going to bed, Mister Rogers wrote a public service announcement that stated, "Some television programs are loud and scary, with people shooting and hitting each other. Well, you can do something about that. When you see scary television like that, you can turn it off. And when you do turn it off, that will show you that you are the strongest of them all. It takes a very strong person to be able to turn off scary TV."[3]

• Sometimes, computer video games will include content that makes a political statement. For example, the 1985 Cold War strategy game *Balance of Power* made an anti-nuclear war statement. Players were supposed to avoid a nuclear war in the game. Knowing that some players might create a nuclear war simply to see some neat computer graphics, the creators made sure that when a nuclear war erupted in the game, a screen would appear that said simply, "You have ignited a nuclear war .... We do not reward failure." Another example of political content occurred in the game *SimCopter*, one of whose creators, Jacques Servin, got fired (in 1996) because he had secretly written computer code that resulted in certain male characters in the game kissing other male characters.[4]

• The Oak Room at the Plaza Hotel in New York was a place where important business lunches were held—and where women weren't permitted unless a man escorted them. On February 12, 1969, Betty Friedan and other members of the National Organization of Women dressed very nicely and headed to the Oak Room. When the manager would not allow them to enter, they marched past him and seated themselves. However, no one would serve them. Because NOW had alerted the media ahead of time, lots of newspapers, radio stations, and television stations were on hand to capture the scene. A few days after the protest, the Oak Room changed its policy and allowed women to dine there without male escorts.[5]

• Not so long ago, gays were regarded as mentally ill; psychiatrists, including Charles Socarides, forced some gays to undergo aversion therapy in which they were shown photographs of nude men, then were electrically shocked or forced to vomit. Some gays were even legally given electroshock treatments. Gay activists fought back, and in 1970 they infiltrated a meeting of the American Psychiatric Association. A film shown at the meeting depicted gays being forced to vomit whenever they saw photographs of nude men. When the film was shown, the gay men infiltrating the meeting waited until photographs of nude men appeared on screen, then they cheered. A few years later, the APA decided that being homosexual was NOT a mental disease. (One wonders if Dr. Socarides ever apologized to the gays he tortured.)[6]

• Vera Cáslavská of Czechoslovakia engaged in an impressive act of activism at the 1968 Olympic Games in Mexico City. The Soviet military had rolled into Czechoslovakia two months earlier, putting an end to free speech. In Mexico City, Ms. Cáslavská won the gold medal in the women's gymnastics all-around competition and received a total of four gold and two silver medals at this Olympics. She shared the gold medal in the floor exercise event with Soviet athlete Larissa Petrik. While the Czech national anthem played, Ms. Cáslavská stood tall and was proud, but when the Soviet national anthem played, she hung her head and was sad. Everyone at the Olympics knew what the Czech citizen was sad about.[7]

• During the Montgomery, Alabama, bus boycott, which lasted 381 days, blacks declined to ride on the city's segregated buses. Instead, they walked, rode in car pools, and took taxis. African-American taxi drivers even lowered their prices to match those offered by the bus company. An African-American minister who worked in the car pool organized by the Montgomery Improvement Association asked an elderly black woman who was walking, "Sister, aren't you getting tired?" She replied, "My soul has been tired for a long time. Now my feet are tired, and my soul is resting." The Supreme Court ruled that the segregated buses were against the Constitution, and the boycott ended in victory for the civil rights workers.[8]

• On June 30, 1966, the third National Conference of State Commissions on the Status of Women was held in Washington, D.C. Betty Friedan attended, along with some other women who planned to ask the government workers attending the commission to treat sex discrimination seriously. Unfortunately, they quickly discovered that the government workers had no intention of listening to them, so during the conference Ms. Friedan and the other women started planning an organization that would take sex discrimination seriously. That organization, which was created under the noses of the government workers who had ignored them, was the National Organization of Women.[9]

• Union organizer Mother Jones knew the effects of child labor at first hand. To learn about working conditions in Southern mills, she had taken jobs at some of them, where she had worked alongside children. Once, she saw heavy machinery tear off one of the fingers of a child employee. Another time, she attended the funeral of an 11-year-old child in Alabama who had died in a factory accident. In 1903, Mother Jones drew attention to the situation of children working in the mills in Philadelphia by having them display their injuries—some children were missing thumbs that had been cut off at work, while other children were missing entire hands that had been cut off at work.[10]

• During World War II, the Japanese occupied Malaysia from January 1942 to August 1945. After the occupation of the town of Seremban, a Japanese executive decided to use a pond to raise ducks; therefore, he ordered that the pond be fenced in, then he released 600 ducklings into the pond. However, the Malaysians did not appreciate the Japanese executive's plans. At the end of two months, only 300 ducklings were still alive, and at the end of three months, only 60 ducklings were still alive. When the Malaysians were questioned about the disappearance of the ducklings, they suggested that the ducklings didn't know how to swim and therefore must have drowned.[11]

• Lithuanians hated being under Soviet domination, and this hatred appeared in their underground humor. In the town square of Kaunas was a statue of Vladimir Lenin with one hand stretched out to the people, and the other hand behind his back. To illustrate life under the Communists, Lithuanians used to place objects in Lenin's hands. In the hand behind Lenin's back was placed a piece of bread, and in the hand stretched out to the people was placed a piece of doggy doo-doo. Also, Lithuanians used to pretend the statue was a scarecrow. Each spring, plants would appear around the statue; Lithuanians had secretly planted the plants.[12]

• Some people may be surprised to learn what the ground in front of the White House contains. When the lover of David Robinson died of AIDS, Mr. Robinson thought of mailing his ashes to the White House to protest the then-administration's lack of action on research to fight AIDS. However, he decided to do a more public act of protest. Together with many other activists, he (and they) carried the ashes of departed loved ones who had died of AIDS and threw them over the fence onto the White House lawn. It was a rainy day, and the rain mixed the ashes with the soil.[13]

• The great dancer Bill Robinson, aka Mr. Bojangles, worked for social change—and even lobbied the President of the United States on one occasion. Mr. Bojangles met President Franklin Delano Roosevelt when the President was working out details of the New Deal. Mr. Bojangles said to President Roosevelt, "By the way, Mr. President, I see you got some kind of New Deal going. Just remember, Mr. President, when you shuffle those cards, just don't overlook those spades."[14]

• In Jerusalem, Myriam Mendilow started Lifeline for the Old, a series of programs for the elderly to give them work and help them earn respect. When she learned that many elderly people in Jerusalem had no health care, she organized a march of elderly people upon the government. Hundreds of elderly people marched to the health ministry at city hall, taking officials by surprise. City and state officials conferred and agreed to work together to provide health care for the elderly.[15]

• Unfortunately, Native Americans often suffer from poverty, alcoholism, high dropout rates, and other evils. Members of the American Indian Movement, an activist organization advocating civil rights for Native Americans, sometimes flew the American flag upside down. This upset many people, but the members of AIM felt that this use of an international distress signal was justified.[16]

• Australians know how to engage in activism. When the Australian prime minister would not apologize to Aborigine peoples because of the removal of Aboriginal children from their homes, 250,000 people in Sydney walked on the Sydney Harbour bridge on May 28, 2000, and a plane above the bridge skywrote the word "Sorry."[17]

• A couple of gay men were passing a women's health clinic when they saw a group of protesters out front. Wanting to do something to support their sisters, the first gay man hugged the second gay man, and then the second gay man kissed the first gay man. They kept on hugging and kissing, and soon the protesters dispersed.[18]

• Abbie Hoffman and his Yippies once showed how greedy and materialistic stock traders could be. They showered dollar bills onto the floor of the New York Stock Exchange, creating chaos and stopping the tickertape as stock traders dove to collect the money.[19]

• Often, people (and courts) feel that mothers should receive custody of children when parents divorce. Some fathers have disputed this, and they sometimes protest by carrying signs that say, "We Demand Women's Equality. Let Men Have Custody."[20]

Advertising

• Heinz baked beans were popular in Great Britain, but consumers bought private-label baked beans at half the price of Heinz baked beans and liked them. And why not? The private-label baked beans were actually Heinz baked beans; the only difference was that the baked beans were packaged under the store's name. To get consumers to buy the expensive Heinz baked beans, Heinz resorted to advertising. A TV commercial showed a haughty English schoolgirl eating Heinz baked beans, then asking her mother, "I wonder ... if I eat Heinz baked beans every day, do you think I could be ... Prime Minister?" Her mother says, "You might, Margaret, you just might." Suddenly, a look of horror comes over the mother's face, and she takes the baked beans away from the girl. In another TV commercial, a boy playing a young Neil Kinnock, leader of the opposition to Prime Minister Margaret Thatcher, is shown eating Heinz baked beans and asking his mother, "If I eat enough baked beans, do you think I could become Prime Minister?" This time, the mother tells the child not to "talk daft. Not a chance in Hell." This was accurate, by the way. Mr. Kinnock tried three times to become Prime Minister, but he failed each time.[21]

• Paid political announcements can backfire. In 1936, this announcement was broadcast on a Yiddish-language radio station: "My dear friends, I would like for you to vote for Wendell Willkie. Willkie is an honest man, a trustworthy man, a gentleman. He loves Jews. Truly a great human being." So far, so good. Unfortunately, after a brief pause, the radio personality said these words: "That was a paid political announcement. I, personally, intend to vote for Roosevelt."[22]

Advice

• After an attempt to remove then-President Mikhail Gorbachev from office in the Soviet Union, many frantic Americans and Soviets went to the American embassy for advice. Some Americans were worried about losing their businesses, and some Soviets were hoping to be allowed to emigrate. An American tour group leader asked for advice, and received the reply to stay out of crowds. Shocked, the American tour group leader asked, "Does that mean I can't go shopping?"[23]

• Texas governor Ann Richards knew how to give advice to teenagers. She once saw a teenager pouring charcoal lighter directly onto a fire, but she did not tell him directly how stupid such an action was; instead, she said, "Honey, if you keep doing that, the fire is going to climb right back up to that can in your hand and explode and give you horrible injuries, and it will just ruin my entire weekend."[24]

AIDS

• AIDS activist Tim Bailey wanted his corpse to be thrown over the fence at the White House in protest of the lack of action in combating AIDS. Of course, that wasn't feasible, so instead he asked that his corpse be carried (in a coffin) in a protest march in Washington, D.C. The political funeral took place in July of 1993. Not surprisingly, the police were against this kind of activism, so a standoff ensued between the living activists and the police, who wouldn't allow the coffin to be removed from the van that had transported it to Washington. Eventually, the police told the activists that in order for them to have a procession, they needed a death certificate and the corpse had to be examined by a coroner. The coroner examined the corpse, and the activists shouted, "ARE YOU SATISFIED? IS HE DEAD ENOUGH? THIS IS WHAT AIDS LOOKS LIKE. ARE YOU PROUD OF YOURSELF?" Eventually, some of the protesters were arrested, and the remaining protesters carried flowers because Mr. Bailey used to fill his backpack with flowers so he could pass them out during Gay Pride parades.[25]

• In the early 1980s, San Francisco AIDS activist Cleve Jones got the idea for the Names Project, also known as the AIDS Memorial

Quilt. In the Names Project, people who wish to honor the memory of a relative, friend, or other loved one who has died of AIDS create a quilt with the loved one's name on it. Many of the quilts are very simple, while others are very complex. Often, the quilts bear mementos of the person being honored—a love letter, a wedding ring, an article of clothing, and so on. Each quilt measures six feet by three feet, which is approximately the size of a grave.[26]

• Penny Raife Durant, the author of *When Heroes Die*, a novel for young people about a man who dies from AIDS, spoke with her younger son about AIDS. The conversation was difficult for her, but the result was good. He told her, "I'm just going to say this once. Now you just listen. I don't intend to have sex before marriage. But if something would happen and I would decide to have sex before marriage, I would use a condom." She then told her son, "That's wonderful. I'm very proud of you."[27]

Alcohol

• In the early part of the 20th century, McLeansboro, Illinois, had a town drunk who showed up bright and early at the town tavern, had a few drinks, then went outside and leaned on one of the porch pillars for an hour, then went back inside for a few more drinks. From opening time to closing time, he would alternate time spent leaning on the pillar with time spent drinking at the bar. One day, he was so drunk that he collapsed near the porch pillar and lay motionless. One of the town's leading citizens walked by, saw the man lying motionless, then went into the tavern and told the proprietor, "Your sign fell down."[28]

• In the summer of 1787, Benjamin Franklin worked hard at the Constitutional Convention in Philadelphia, but in the evenings he went to a tavern for rest and relaxation. Another delegate, a teetotaler, decided to convince Mr. Franklin to give up his evil ways by showing him a demonstration of the effects of alcohol. He got two glasses and filled one with rum and another with water, then he put a worm in each glass. The worm in the water began to swim, but the worm in the rum quickly died. "What does that teach you?" asked the teetotaler. Mr. Franklin replied, "If you have worms, drink rum."[29]

• At Kenwood in London is a house that has been turned into a museum. The house was almost destroyed by a mob during the Gordon Riots of 1780, but its steward saved it. Tired from its rioting, the mob decided to stop at the Spaniards Inn before burning the house at Kenwood. The tavern keeper sent a message to the Kenwood steward, warning him of the danger. Thinking quickly, the steward sent for help, and also sent a barrel of ale to the tavern keeper to keep the mob drunk until help arrived. The steward's plan worked, and the house at Kenwood was saved.[30]

• When the Eighteenth Amendment—which made Prohibition legal—was repealed, citizens celebrated across the United States. In Freeport, Long Island, members of the American Legion formed a firing squad and shot a dummy labeled "Prohibition." In Milwaukee, a man walked into a newly re-opened hot spot called Heine's. The bartender asked if he wanted a beer, and the man replied, "Yes, please. Make mine legal."[31]

Bathrooms

• Lord Louis Mountbatten was understandably happy when he received a prototype model of a new aircraft carrier that he felt could help Great Britain and its allies win World War II. He was eager to show the prototype model to Prime Minister Winston Churchill, and so he asked, "Where is the Old Man?" The reply came back that the Old Man was taking a bath, so Lord Mountbatten took a great liberty and entered the Prime Minister's bathroom, where Churchill was soaking in the tub. Fortunately, Churchill was also happy to see the prototype model, and according to Lord Mountbatten, he played with it in the tub "as if it were a rubber duck."[32]

• Members of royalty get special privileges. The Duke of Windsor occasionally ate at Le Pavillon in New York. Whenever he went to the bathroom, the proprietor of the restaurant, Henri Soule, guarded the door—no one was allowed to see the Duke of Windsor in the bathroom.[33]

Celebrities

• While in Yugoslavia, movie star Kirk Douglas wanted to meet President Josip Broz Tito, so he paid a visit to the British embassy, where he met the British ambassador, who told him, "My boy, I've been here for six weeks and have yet to see Tito. You don't stand a chance." The very next day, Tito sent his very own private plane to take Mr. Douglas to Lubiana, where the two men met. When Mr. Douglas returned, the British ambassador asked him how such an amazing event could happen. Mr. Douglas replied, "Mr. Ambassador, how many movies have *you* made?"[34]

• Satiric songwriter Tom Lehrer, who wrote "The Vatican Rag," has his share of fans. At a party hosted by John Kenneth Galbraith, he and Jackie Kennedy were introduced to a woman who ignored Jackie, turned to Mr. Lehrer, and cried in astonishment, "Tom Lehrer!"[35]

Children

• Children who are refugees often have had tough childhoods. One 12-year-old refugee girl from El Salvador said, "I have never had any toys. All I've ever done is work." A boy living in a refugee camp in Thailand helped his family survive by going to a cemetery and looking for mint. He traded the mint for cane sugar, which he then traded for rice for his family and him to eat.[36]

• The BBC's Jenni Murray recognizes the influence that Margaret Thatcher had as the first woman to serve as British Prime Minister. When the news came that Ms. Thatcher would be replaced by John Major, Ms. Murray's nine-year-old asked her, "Mum, is that right? I thought prime minister was a woman's job."[37]

Clothing

• The first time Margaret Bourke-White wanted to take Mahatma Gandhi's photograph, she had to show that she knew how to use a spinning wheel before she was allowed to meet the great man. At the time, the British took cotton from India, shipped it to Great Britain where it was made into clothing, then shipped it back to India to be sold. To create jobs for the citizens of India, Gandhi wanted them to weave the cotton into cloth. After taking a quick lesson in spinning, Ms. Bourke-White was able to demonstrate sufficient competence to see Gandhi and to take a world-famous photograph of him.[38]

• Ann Richards, former governor of Texas, did not put up with BS. Going through an airport metal detector while she was wearing underpants with metal snaps, she set off an alarm and the security guard wanted to take her to a private area where Ms. Richards's underpants could be investigated thoroughly. However, Ms. Richards was late for her flight, so she told the security guard, "I will take off my pants here and now—right here." The security guard decided to let her board her flight without any further annoyance.[39]

• President George W. Bush was widely despised both at home and abroad. In Seattle, Washington, a manufacturer of backpacks and laptop bags doubled sales because its products have a tiny laundry label that says, "*Nous sommes desoles que notre president soit un idiot. Nous n'avons pas vote pour lui.*" Translated from the French, the label says, "We are sorry that our president is an idiot. We did not vote for him."[40]

Crime

• After a rebellion in Mexico failed in 1910, its leaders fled to the United States, where they were imprisoned under false charges. Union organizer Mother Jones spoke to President William Howard Taft and asked that the rebel leaders be pardoned. President Taft said, "Now, Mother, the trouble lies here: if I put the pardoning power in your hands, there would be no one left in the jails." Mother Jones replied, "I'm not so sure of that, Mr. President. ... A lot of those who are in would be out, but a lot of those who are out would be in." President Taft laughed, and later he did as Mother Jones had asked and pardoned the rebel leaders. For such actions as this, Mother Jones became a hero to many people in Mexico as well as in the United States. (Of course, such actions meant that some people in both countries regarded her as a very dangerous woman.)[41]

• In 1938, Margaret Bourke-White investigated problems in New Jersey's Jersey City, which was run by its corrupt mayor, "Boss" Frank Hague. He insisted that she be accompanied at all times by members of the local police, who were as corrupt as he was and who served as his private army. However, Ms. Bourke-White managed to elude the police escort one day, and she succeeded in taking photographs of a young girl staying home from school to help her family make money by making paper flowers. Ms. Bourke-White gave the most important film to one of her assistants, who smuggled it out of the city. This was fortunate because the police caught up with her and ripped some other film from her camera. The film that was smuggled out of Jersey City proved the existence of child labor there.[42]

• The late Jesse Helms, a North Carolina Senator, once threatened President Bill Clinton, saying that if the President ever came to North Carolina, he had better have a bodyguard with him. Michael Moore, director of *Roger and Me*, was interested enough in the threat to have his researcher telephone the Secret Service in Washington, D.C., and make a complaint. During the call, the researcher discovered that the Secret Service was taking the threat seriously. After Senator Helms made his threat, the Secret Service interviewed him. Senator Helms' name appeared on a list that the Secret Service keeps of people who have threatened the President.[43]

• When Julius Caesar was a young man, pirates captured him and held him for ransom as he sailed for the Greek island of Rhodes. The sailors told him that they would ransom him for twenty talents—a very large sum of money. Caesar laughed at them, said that he was more valuable than that, and told them to ransom him for fifty talents. He also freely insulted the pirates and said that he would crucify them, but the pirates laughed at this threat. After Caesar had been ransomed, he organized a fleet of ships to hunt down the pirates. As he had promised, he crucified them.[44]

• Thaddeus Stevens once told President Abraham Lincoln not to make any deals with Simon Cameron. When President Lincoln asked Mr. Stevens whether he thought that Mr. Cameron was a thief, Mr. Stevens replied, "I don't think that he would steal a red-hot stove." Word of Mr. Stevens' comment got to Mr. Cameron, and he demanded that Mr. Stevens make a retraction. Therefore, Mr. Stevens told President Lincoln, "He is very mad and made me promise to retract. I will now do so. I believe I told you he would *not* steal a red-hot stove. I now take that back."[45]

• Some convicts are wise guys. In 1986, police in Green Bay, Wisconsin, placed an order for license plates for their unmarked police cars. Wisconsin convicts made the license plates, and on each license plate they put the initials "PD"—short for "Police Department." Deputy Police Chief Robert Langan rejected the license plates and sent them back, saying, "They were a dead giveaway."[46]

• At a time of an epidemic of sexual assaults against women in Israel, the Israeli cabinet discussed instituting a curfew for women, thus not allowing women to be outside after a certain time. Israeli politician Golda Meir objected, "But it's the men who are attacking the women. If there's a curfew, let the men stay at home, not the women."[47]

• During Prohibition, many law enforcement officers were corrupt. One speakeasy in New York City was made with two entrances. After making a raid for the benefit of public relations, the federal agents would lock one door but not the other, with the result that as soon as the federal agents had left, the speakeasy was once again open for business.[48]

• As a Chicago journalist, Eugene Field wrote the truth when he stated in an article, "Half the aldermen in the city are crooks." The aldermen were not pleased with the article, and they demanded a retraction, so Mr. Field wrote, "Half the aldermen in the city are not crooks."[49]

15

Chapter 2: From Dance to Good Deeds

Dance

• Things that are very good can be used for things that are very evil. For example, during the Middle Passage across the Atlantic Ocean the crews of slave ships would bring slaves up on deck to dance. This practice was known as "dancing the slaves." The captains of the slave ships believed that the dancing would keep the slaves looking healthy so that they could be sold for a high price. Sometimes, the slaves were forced to sing as they danced. As you would expect, the songs were mournful laments about being forced into exile.[50]

• Politicians often do not understand art. Martha Graham choreographed *Phaedra*, and Isamu Noguchi created a bed to be used as a prop on stage. The bed bothered Congressman Peter Freylinghuysen of New Jersey, but Ms. Graham informed him that the bed was uncomfortable, only one person could lie on it at a time, and it was totally unsuited for any kind of amorous activity, although the congressman was welcome to give it a try. Ms. Graham then added, "I think eroticism is a lovely thing. Don't you?"[51]

Death

• While in prison awaiting her execution, Marie Antoinette, Queen of France, was given no privacy. Her jailors even watched her dress and undress. Even while she was dressing on the morning of her execution, the jailors watched her—until she cried out, "In the name of God and decency, I beg you give me some privacy!" She did not object when the executioner cut off her long hair (short hair helps ensure the guillotine does its works quickly), but she became upset when she had to ride to the place of execution in a cattle cart rather than a coach. A crowd watched her ride in the cattle cart, and a mother held up her little daughter to see the doomed Queen of France. Not knowing what was going on, the little girl blew her a kiss, and Ms. Antoinette smiled briefly. Standing before the guillotine, Ms. Antoinette accidentally stepped on her executioner's hand, and said, "Pardon me, monsieur. I did not do it on purpose." Those were her last words.[52]

• In January of 1996, college student Mark Oppenheimer interviewed Reverend William Sloane Coffin, Jr., in Appleton, Wisconsin. Part of the interview took place in a cemetery where Reverend Coffin let his dog run free. The dog stopped at the grave of Senator Joseph McCarthy, who had destroyed lives with innuendo during the 1950s. Lifting its leg, the dog peed on Senator McCarthy's tombstone. Reverend Coffin joked, "Our daily ritual." As a leftist, Reverend Coffin was outspoken against the Vietnam War, creating quite a lot of controversy. He was Chaplain at Yale, and Yale President Kingman Brewster once asked him, "Bill, do you know how much time I spend defending you?" Reverend Coffin replied, "As much time as you spend defending me to the right, I spend defending you to the left."[53]

• One way of resisting oppression is to make jokes. Paul Joseph Goebbels, who was Propaganda Minister under Adolf Hitler, died and was given his choice of either Heaven or Hell. To aid him in his decision, he was given a tour of each after-life destination. In Heaven, he saw people enjoying a quiet, spiritual existence. In Hell, he saw a noisy bar with lots of music, dancing, and women. To Goebbels, the decision was a no-brainer: He chose Hell. After he made his decision, Satan picked him up, carried him past the bar into a dungeon in which were pots of boiling oil, then threw him into one of the pots. "Wait a minute," Goebbels protested. "What about the bar, the music, the dancing, and the women?" Satan replied, "That was propaganda."[54]

• Maury Wills was known for his speed, base running, and ability to steal bases in major-league baseball. In 1961, in a playoff series with Mr. Wills' Dodgers, the Giants needed to find a way to keep Mr. Wills from getting a big lead. They solved the problem by pouring water around first base, creating something resembling a bog. In 1968, Mr. Wills was playing for Pittsburgh when Bobby Kennedy was assassinated. Mr. Wills respected the Kennedys, and he asked to sit out a game because of Mr. Kennedy's death. The Pirates refused to give him permission to sit out the game, although most other major-league teams had cancelled their games. Mr. Wills sat out the game anyway.[55]

• When the *Titanic* sank on April 15, 1912, most of the people on board died. Only 705 passengers and crew survived, and 1,503 people died. Because of the disaster, laws improving safety at sea were passed. Ships at sea were required to have a radio operator on duty 24 hours a day. The United States formed the International Ice Patrol to keep track of icebergs and give information about their positions to ships near them. In addition, because the *Titanic* had fewer than half the number of lifeboats needed to save its passengers and crew, a new law required ships to have enough lifeboats to save everybody on board.[56]

• In 399 B.C.E., the ancient Greek philosopher Socrates was accused of corrupting the young men of Athens and of denying the reality of the gods. After being found guilty, he was sentenced to die. In prison, he drank the poison hemlock he was given, and in this way he was executed. Later, following the death of Alexander the Great, Athenians wanted to get rid of people such as the philosopher Aristotle, who had been associated with Alexander. Rather than standing trial, being found guilty, and being sentenced to die, Aristotle went into exile, saying that he did not want the Athenians to sin twice against philosophy.[57]

• Leonidas and 300 Spartans died at the pass of Thermopylae in a successful attempt to slow the advance of the invading Persian army and give the Greeks time to raise an army. Hearing that the arrows of the Persians would be shot so quickly and so densely that they would blot out the sun, the Spartan Dienekes said, "Good. Then we will fight in the shade." The Spartans knew that they would die defending the pass. The morning of their final battle, Leonidas told his men, "Eat well, for tonight we dine in Hades."[58]

• During World War I, a friend of flying ace Eddie Rickenbacker died after jumping without a parachute from a burning plane. Therefore, Mr. Rickenbacker tried to get the government to issue parachutes to pilots, but the government refused. Why? It said that if pilots had parachutes, they would parachute to safety, leaving crippled but expensive aircraft to crash. But if the pilots did not have parachutes, they would fight to land their expensive aircraft.[59]

• Senator Allen Ellender, a Democrat from Louisiana, was a tireless critic of subcommittees, believing that they go on long after they are needed and that their staff proliferates needlessly. After he died, a note he had written was found among his belongings: "If there is a life hereafter, I want to come back as a standing subcommittee in the Senate, because they never fade out."[60]

• Herbert Hoover once joked that he believed that the President of the United States should be allowed to hang two men a year without having to give any sort of explanation. A friend asked if two men per year would be enough. "Perhaps not," replied President Hoover, "but I could get word to 20 or 30 that they were being considered for the honor."[61]

• Franklin Delano Roosevelt almost did not become President of the United States. As he was speaking in Miami, Florida, a would-be assassin fired a gun at him, but missed him and hit Anton Cermak, the mayor of Chicago, instead. Mr. Cermak died a few days later, but not before telling Mr. Roosevelt, "I'm glad it was me instead of you."[62]

• After Owen Brewster died, fellow Maine politician Percival P. Baxter stopped to visit his grave. Mr. Baxter's chauffeur, Joseph Lee, remarked that Mr. Baxter was making quite a graceful gesture toward a former political enemy, but Mr. Baxter told him, "No, I just wanted to be sure the SOB was really dead."[63]

• In 1853, famous detective Allan Pinkerton was shot twice as he walked home. The perpetrator had tried to shoot him in the back twice, but Mr. Pinkerton had a habit of walking with one arm behind his back. This habit probably saved his life since the bullets entered his arm and not his torso.[64]

• Joseph Hillstrom (Joe Hill) was a labor organizer who was convicted of a murder on circumstantial evidence and executed. The day before he faced the firing squad, he sent a telegram to another labor organizer, advising, "Don't waste any time in mourning. Organize!"[65]

• Sharon Salzberg once had a meditation student who had been a child in a part of Europe that was occupied by the Nazis. Once, a Nazi soldier pointed a gun at her chest, and she thought, "You may be able to kill my body, but you can't kill me."[66]

• Frances Perkins, Secretary of Labor under Franklin Delano Roosevelt, had a feisty grandfather. At age 104, he ordered a new pair of boots and requested that the cobbler do an especially good job on them because "very few men die after the age of 99."[67]

• Former Senator Dennis Chavez, a Democrat from New Mexico, once stood and smiled as an orchestra played a song. Afterward, he learned that the orchestra had been playing, "I'll Be Glad When You're Dead, You Rascal, You."[68]

Education

• Kate Barnhart became an activist for AIDS at a young age. As a member of ACT UP, she has even been arrested a few times. When she applied for admission for college, she was asked to write an essay on her "most positive educational experience," and instead of writing about such things as a favorite biology course, she wrote about her experiences as an activist. Ms. Barnhart says, "I was rejected by ten schools. But I figured I didn't want to go to any school that wouldn't accept me for who I am."[69]

• During World War II, despite rules against education, Jews still opened and ran schools in the ghettos. Some schools were disguised as workshops or soup kitchens, and some teachers taught a few students at home. Whenever the Nazis came around a teacher's home, the teacher would pretend to be teaching students such things as how to make military uniforms and shoes for the Nazis instead of what they were really teaching: Hebrew, literature, mathematics, etc.[70]

• This anecdote is probably an urban legend, but it is funny. Following World War II, GIs who had not completed high school were allowed to return to high school to get their degree. Of course, these GIs were a lot older than the other students. One G.I. received his report card, then asked a teacher, "Who do you want me to get to sign it: my mother, my wife, or my daughter?"[71]

• When Barbara Bush, wife of President George H. W. Bush, was asked to speak to the graduating class of Wellesley College, many of the graduates did not want her to speak. They protested, "To honor Barbara Bush as a commencement speaker is to honor a woman who has gained recognition through the achievements of her husband, which contradicts what we have been taught over our years at Wellesley."[72]

• During detention in a Brooklyn school auditorium filled with unruly kids, a kid shouted, "Give me liberty or give me death!" The teacher had her back turned and did not see who was doing the shouting, so she asked, "Who said that?" The kids knew the answer, and several replied, "Patrick Henry."[73]

• At Harrow House, a housemaster was confronted with a group of unruly youngsters whom he didn't how to control. He said in despair, "I don't know what to do with you boys." A small boy by the name of Winston Churchill replied, "Please, sir, teach us."[74]

• At Duke University in 1992, feminists staged a memorable protest against sexual assaults. Bands of feminists lay in wait for solitary men, then "assaulted" them by plastering their bodies with bright pink stickers that said, "Gotcha!"[75]

Food

• The young can be much more cynical than the aged. For example, President Richard M. Nixon invited Rabbi Morris N. Kertzer to attend a conference on drug abuse, and so the President's secretary called

Rabbi Kertzer and said, "We understand you keep kosher. What would you like for lunch?" The older people to whom Rabbi Kertzer related the story were impressed that President Nixon would show such sensitivity to a rabbi's dietary needs, but the 10th-grade students to whom Rabbi Kertzer related the story were upset. One student explained why: "The White House keeps a file on you."[76]

• During World War II, food could be hard to get in Nazi-occupied France. Some animals were hidden in the woods to keep the Nazis from finding them, and a black market arose in meat. The mother of ballet student Violette Verdy was able to buy half a pig with cash and Violette's bicycle. After the pig was slaughtered in the woods, half of it was hidden in a laundry basket and smuggled past Nazi sentries to Violette and her mother. Violette learned many, many ways to prepare parts of a pig for eating.[77]

• According to legend, emperor Shen Nung discovered tea in China in the year 2737 B.C.E. when he stopped to take refreshment under a wild tea tree while he was traveling. As a health measure, he boiled water before drinking it, and some leaves from the tea tree fell into the water, making its color brown and its smell inviting. He enjoyed the drink, and soon it became popular throughout China.[78]

Free Speech

• While hosting a talk show on CBS from 1969-1972, Merv Griffin had many guests who spoke out against the very unpopular Vietnam War. CBS wanted him to be "balanced," and CBS officials pointed out in a memo to him these facts: "In the past six weeks, thirty-four antiwar statements have been made on your show and only one pro-war statement, by John Wayne." Mr. Griffin responded, "Find me someone as famous as John Wayne who supports the war and I'll book him." The earliest person to speak out against the Vietnam War—before the war became unpopular—was the philosopher Bertrand Russell, who said that he wanted the United States to "give up the habit of invading peaceful countries and torturing them." People were outraged by Lord Russell's opinion, but Mr. Griffin defended Lord Russell's right to free speech: "… nothing would be easier for me than to book this show with people who have ideas that are carbon copies of my own, or no ideas at all. But I don't think it's an easy world or that my primary responsibility on this program is to take it easy. You'll continue on this show to see people of every persuasion who have hard things to say, and I don't think you can get at any truth without hammering out on the anvil of everyone's right to disagree."[79]

• Right-wing rocker Ted Nugent, famous for the song "Cat Scratch Fever," is also famous for being a draft dodger. During the Vietnam War, he did not want to serve his country, so he figured out a way to avoid the draft. According to an article by Richard Roeper, aptly titled "Facing a draft, Nugent bravely wet his pants," Mr. Nugent dispensed with personal hygiene for a few weeks before his military physical, and when he showed up for his examination, he was wearing urine-soaked and feces-encrusted clothing. The dodge worked; he did not have to serve his country. Mr. Nugent bravely uses his freedom of speech that so many soldiers fought for; for example, he has bravely used his freedom of speech to criticize women and African-Americans. Mr. Nugent has referred to Hillary Clinton as a "worthless b*tch" and to Dianne Feinstein as a "worthless wh*re," and he has called Barack Obama "a piece of [expletive deleted]."[80]

• A citizen of the USSR traveled to the US to live, and reporters interviewed him. The reporters asked such questions about the USSR as "How abundant are goods?" and "How are prices?" and "How is the standard of living?" To each of these questions, the man replied, "One can't complain." Finally, the reporters asked why he had chosen to live in the US instead of in the USSR. He replied, "In the US, one can complain."[81]

Gambling

• The "tributes" given to the late Ohio House Speaker Vern Riffe as reported on Columbus (Ohio) TV news after he died in 1997 were shocking. The stories the tribute-speakers told about Vern, a Republican, were meant to be amusing anecdotes, but instead they revealed him to be a total jerk. For example, according to one story, Vern was gambling on a plane with some other politicians. He was losing, so when the plane arrived at the airport, he ordered the pilot to circle the airport so he could win back his money. The plane circled the airport so many times that the pilot was getting nervous, so one of the politicians on the plane told Vern that he would pay him the money Vern had lost just so the plane would land.[82]

• As a young lawyer practicing in Illinois, Abraham Lincoln once made an agreement to trade horses with a judge, with the agreement being that each person would be satisfied with whatever horse the other brought to be traded. The judge arrived first, leading a sorry, swayback specimen of a horse, then Mr. Lincoln arrived, carrying a sawhorse on his shoulder. Mr. Lincoln placed the sawhorse on the ground, looked over the judge's horse, then told the judge, "This is the first time I ever got the worst of it in a horse trade."[83]

Gays and Lesbians

• Andrew Tobias, personal finance expert, Treasurer of the Democratic National Committee, and gay man, knows quite a few politicians, including gay and lesbian politicians. For example, he knows two lesbians who in 2007 were first-year legislators in a state that he declines to name, and some of the friendly straight male politicians with whom they work and who know that they are lesbians will sometimes call them on one of the telephones rigged up in the legislative chamber. Some calls are about important legislative matters, but occasionally a straight male politician will call the lesbian legislators to inform them that an especially good-looking woman is in the gallery. One day, the Fox News correspondent was especially pretty, so the lesbians received a telephone call and of course they wanted to get a good look at the especially pretty Fox News correspondent. One lesbian's view was blocked, so she half-rose out of her seat to get a better view. The Speaker thought that she was rising because of official business, so he asked her, "[F]or what purpose does the gentlelady from [wherever] rise?" Embarrassed, she sat down again; however, Mr. Tobias likes to think about an alternative ending to this story. In his version, the lesbian legislator stands up and says, "Mr. Speaker, I rise to get a better look at the correspondent from Fox News."[84]

• In Colorado, voters had to decide whether to pass a proposal to amend the state constitution to remove legal protection for gays and lesbians. Of course, homosexuals encouraged people to vote 'no' to keep the proposed amendment from becoming law, while bigots encouraged people to vote 'yes' to pass the amendment. Lesbian humorist Ellen Orleans made her contribution to the pro-gay effort by calling voters. One voter, as soon as she heard why Ms. Orleans was calling, said firmly, "I don't like gays, so I'm voting 'no.'" Ms. Orleans wrestled with a moral dilemma for a moment, then thanked the woman for her time and hung up.[85]

• Gay men and lesbians have adopted the pink triangle as a symbol of solidarity, but the pink triangle was first used by the Nazis in 1937 to identify homosexual prisoners in concentration camps. Other identifying symbols for concentration camp inmates were yellow triangles for Jews, purple triangles for Jehovah's Witnesses, brown triangles for Gypsies, red triangles for Communists, blue triangles for illegal emigrés, and black triangles for "asocials" (a group which may have included lesbians)—this is compelling evidence that the Nazis hated everybody, although they especially hated the Jews.[86]

• Will Shank is a gay man, and he was understandably irate when he saw an SUV bearing the bumper sticker "MARRIAGE = MAN + WOMAN," so he told the driver of the SUV, who was in a store, "That's my family in this red car," pointing to his husband and their daughter. Then he added, "And you're a self-righteous b*tch." Her eyes got wide as she realized that she was talking to a gay man, then she ran back to her SUV. As she ran, he called after her, "You put your politics on your car, so you asked for it."[87]

• In the days before Stonewall, lesbians sometimes passed as men. Trudy Genovese knew a lesbian couple, one of whom passed as a man. To make the deception work, the passing lesbian even wore men's underwear because this was in the days when only rich people had washing machines and dryers, and almost everyone hung their laundry on an outdoor clothesline. The couple certainly did not want the neighbors to notice that only women's underwear hung on the line.[88]

• The first American soldier to be drummed out of the Army for being gay was Lt. Gothold Frederick. On March 11, 1778, at Valley Forge, his sword was broken over his head, and he was escorted out of camp to slow drumming. In 1957, the Crittenden Report, commissioned by the United States Army, stated that the presence of gay soldiers did not have a negative effect on troop morale, thus undercutting the main reason for drumming gay soldiers out of the military.[89]

• White-sheeted hoodlums of the White Legion—a Southern California version of the Ku Klux Klan—beat up homosexual couple William Haines and James Shields long ago. Because of this experience, the two men formed an aversion to white sheets. Fortunately, Mr. Haines was an interior decorator, so he used his expertise to create what may have been the first-ever color-coordinated sheet sets.[90]

• The United Kingdom's first openly gay Member of Parliament was Chris Smith, who was elected in 1983 and represented a borough of London. After Mr. Smith came out publicly, all of his fellow Labour Party members of the House of Commons signed a petition in support of him—not one declined to sign.[91]

• Lesbian humorist Ellen Orleans discovered that it's very easy to be considered an activist at a big corporation. After accepting a corporate job, she put a Gay Pride flyer over her desk and immediately her co-workers assumed that she was a militant homosexual activist.[92]

Generals

• General Dwight David Eisenhower refused to pass the buck. He was prepared to take the blame should the Allied invasion on D-day fail. On the eve of D-day, he wrote this note that is now in the National Archives: "Our landings in the Cherbourg-Havre area have failed to gain a satisfactory foothold, and I have withdrawn the troops. My decision to attack at this time and place was based upon the best information available. The troops, the air and navy did all their bravery and devotion to duty could do. If any blame or fault attaches to the attempt, it is mine alone." Fortunately, the Allies were victorious and General Eisenhower did not need to take the blame for failure.[93]

• General Maxwell Taylor decided to discontinue varsity fencing at West Point, and he needed to come up with a reason for his decision when the fencers complained to him. His first excuse was, "Frankly, gentlemen, it's the cost." The fencers laughed, knowing that the cost was approximately $6,000—nothing to the military. His second excuse was, "Frankly, gentlemen, it's the lack of facilities." Again, everyone laughed, knowing that West Point had the best fencing facility in the United States. His third and final excuse was, "Gentlemen, fencing is a sport for intellectuals, and we don't want intellectuals in the army."[94]

• General Ulysses S. Grant showed kindness to General Robert E. Lee and the defeated Confederate soldiers at Appomattox, allowing them to depart, go home, and begin the work of reconstructing their homes and land. General Lee never forgot that kindness, and when a faculty member of Washington College criticized General Grant, General Lee, who was then the president of Washington College, told the faculty member, "Sir, if you presume ever again to speak disrespectfully of General Grant in my presence, either you or I will sever his connection with this university."[95]

• General George Washington was once traveling in a carriage on a narrow street where he overtook a farmer with a load of hay. The farmer was traveling very slowly, so the General's aides told the farmer that he was holding up General Washington and that he would have to move off the side of the road and let the General pass. The farmer disliked the tone of voice the aides were using, so he told them that he had as much right to the use of the road as General Washington had. When the aides reported to General Washington what the farmer had said, he replied, "So he has."[96]

Good Deeds

• The hero of syndicated columnist Susan Estrich is Judge J. Skelly Wright, a thoroughly decent man who became a hero simply by being just in his judicial decisions. For example, the case *Williams v. Walker-Thomas Furniture Store* concerned a furniture store that took advantage of impoverished African-Americans by offering credit at very high interest rates and by repossessing furniture as soon as a payment was missed. Of course, The Uniform Commercial Code prohibits commercial transactions that take unconscionable advantage of the consumer, and Walker-Thomas Furniture Store was doing exactly that. Judge Wright ruled against Walker-Thomas Furniture Store, thus incurring the hatred of many business owners. He also made decisions that integrated the New Orleans school system and allowed black students to enroll in the Louisiana State University law school, thus incurring the hatred of the Ku Klux Klan. Ms. Estrich wrote in a column honoring Judge Wright, "The Klan burned crosses on his lawn so often his son once told me that when his parents went out, his dad told him to just ignore them unless they got too close to the house, in which case he should call the fire department."[97]

• During the struggle between the White Army (anti-Communists) and the Red Army (Communists) in Ukraine following World War I, Jews were persecuted by both sides. A platoon of the White Army stopped the train that Isaac Abramson was traveling on, and the soldiers robbed and beat him, then left him by the railroad tracks, unconscious. Fortunately, a dog found him and stayed by him. When the dog's owner came looking for the dog, he found Mr.

Abramson, had him carried to his home, and took care of him. Later, Mr. Abramson, his wife (Manya), and their son (Valodya) emigrated to the United States and safety.[98]

• Vinoba Bhave worked with Mahatma Gandhi to win independence for India, and after the assassination of Gandhi, he was regarded as Gandhi's spiritual successor. He started the *bhoodan yagna*, or land-gift movement. Walking throughout India, he asked wealthy people to donate land to poor people. Many people did this, donating millions of acres of land to be used by the poor. In one case, a poor man gave one-thirteenth of an acre of land because he had started a job at a factory. Vinoba Bhave returned the land, saying that the man was poor and ought to be given land instead of donating it.[99]

• During the Holocaust, many people risked their lives to save Jews. Monsignor Jules-Gérard Saliège, the archbishop of Toulouse, France, wrote a pastoral letter opposing the deportation of Jews by the Vichy government. The letter said, "Jews are men. Jews are women. They form part of the family of mankind. They are our brothers, a fact that Christians must not forget." The letter became known as the Saliège Bomb, and it inspired many Christians to rescue Jews.[100]

Chapter 3: From Hitler to Photography

Hitler

• On April 24, 1915, the Turks began to commit genocide against the Armenian people because the Armenians lived both in Turkey and in Russia. The Russians were the enemy of Turkey, and the Turks feared that the Armenians supported the Russians. By the time the Turks were defeated in 1918, they had killed over a million Armenians, and in the famine that followed the end of the war, hundreds of thousands more Armenians starved to death. Should such atrocities be remembered, or is it better to forget them? Adolf Hitler provides the answer to that question. When he decided to engage in genocide, some people told him that they were worried about world opinion. Hitler responded, "Who still talks nowadays of the extermination of the Armenians?"[101]

• One of the biggest upsets in Olympics history occurred in 1936 when the anchor of the German women's 4 x 100 women's relay team dropped the baton on the final leg of the race, thereby losing her team's big lead and allowing the United States team, anchored by fleet-footed Helen Stephens, to win. The other three relay team members gathered around Ilse Dorffeldt, who had dropped the baton, and tried to comfort her. One person who showed sympathy is someone you may not expect to be capable of sympathy. Relay team member Emmy Albus said much later (over 50 years later!), "I know this sounds strange, but Hitler was very sympathetic. The next day he sent us all flowers."[102]

• The Three Stooges—Jews all—showed courage in 1939 and 1940 by mocking Hitler and the Nazis before doing that was encouraged. (Before Pearl Harbor, the Hays Office discouraged the making of anti-Nazi propaganda films.) The Three Stooges' *You Nazty Spy!* was released in January 1940 and their *I'll Never Heil Again* was released in July 1941. *You Nazty Spy!* was set in the Kingdom of Moronica, and in *I'll Never Heil Again* Curly's Field Marshall Herring reports to the Hitler character, "We bombed 56 hospitals, 85 schools, 42 kindergartens, 4 cemeteries, and other vital military objects."[103]

• As Adolf Hitler was rising to power, a teacher asked her young pupils what they would like to be if their father was Hitler. One child wanted to be a U-boat captain. Another wanted to be a Field Marshall. A third wanted to be a general. The lone Jewish child spoke up, "If Hitler were my father, I would want to be an orphan."[104]

Holocaust

• During the Holocaust, some Jewish groups fought Nazi tyranny through armed uprisings; in addition, another way of resisting the Nazis was simply to remain human and to follow one's religion despite cruel and inhuman conditions. Margarine placed in a potato peeling sometimes served as a Sabbath candle; however, when even that was unavailable, Jews made the blessing of the Sabbath candles on the electric lights of the concentration camps. At the Plaszów work camp, the scholar Mendel Brachfeld smuggled in a pair of *tefillin* for use during prayer. Jews stood in line to wear the *tefillin* and say prayers. On Yom Kippur, Jews at the work camp recited the Kol Nidre and other prayers while working despite the grave danger of doing this. Also at the Plaszów work camp, three mattresses and some branches served to make a *sukka* for Succoth, the Jewish religious festival. Even in their final moments before death, some Jews were able to resist the Nazis. One girl managed to slap a Nazi guard just before the Nazis murdered her. An old woman succeeded in comforting and in making a crying child laugh just before the Nazis murdered them. The form of resistance that most shocked the Nazis was something that they could not understand. Just before the Nazis murdered them, some Jews danced with joy, knowing that they were about to enter the Kingdom of God.[105]

• In Warsaw, Poland, where many Jews lived, the Nazis herded all the Jews to live in a ghetto. Emanuel Ringelblum experienced life in the Warsaw Ghetto, where the Nazis did everything in their power to murder the Jewish inhabitants, and he was determined to let the world know what the Jews suffered. He and other historians started a group called the *Oneg Shabbat* Circle. (In Hebrew, *oneg Shabbat* means "Sabbath joy.") They recorded the daily activities and extraordinary events of life in the Warsaw Ghetto, and the manuscripts were placed in milk cans and tin boxes and buried. In 1946, some of the manuscripts were recovered; in 1950, the remaining manuscripts were recovered. The manuscripts reveal horrifying details of the results of the genocide practiced by the Nazis. For example, Jewish children grew so used to seeing dead people that they played a game in which they tickled a corpse.[106]

• Swedish diplomat Raoul Wallenberg saved at least 20,000 Jews in Hungary during World War II, and he may have saved as many as 100,000 Jews, but Soviet soldiers thought that he might be a spy, and so he spent the last years of his life in a Soviet prison. In 1948, a sculpture of Saint George slaying a dragon was supposed to be unveiled in Saint Stephen's Park in Budapest. On the base of the sculpture appeared Mr. Wallenberg's image and this dedication: "This memorial is our silent and eternal gratitude to him and should always remind us of his enduring humanity in a period of inhumanity." The sculpture was put in the park before its unveiling, but the day the sculpture was supposed to be unveiled, spectators saw nothing but an empty space where the sculpture had been. Soviet soldiers had taken away the sculpture during the night.[107]

• A Nazi soldier who had a glass eye went to the Warsaw ghetto to get the child of a Jewish mother so that the child could be sent to a death camp. The mother begged for mercy, and the Nazi soldier told her, "If you can guess which of my eyes is artificial, I'll give you your child." The mother guessed correctly, and the Nazi soldier asked her how she had been able to guess which of his eyes was artificial. The mother replied, "The eye that looks more human than the other one is artificial."[108]

Husbands and Wives

• For a while, Allen Pinkerton and his wife, Joan, lived in Montreal, Canada, but soon Mr. Pinkerton had earned enough money to buy them passage on a ship sailing through the Great Lakes to Chicago, Illinois. He wanted to leave that very day, but Joan told him that she had put a down payment on a hat and she wanted to wait for a few days so she could buy the hat and take it to Chicago. Mr. Pinkerton ranted for a while, then he gave in and agreed to stay in Montreal for a few more days. It's a good thing the Pinkertons stayed. The ship they would have sailed on sank with total loss of life after a boiler exploded. Thereafter, Mr. Pinkerton agreed that his wife could do as she liked about bonnets.[109]

• Paula Ben-Gurion was married to David Ben-Gurion, the Prime Minister of Israel. Once, she was too busy to go shopping, so she asked an armed sentry to run to the store for her. The armed sentry explained that he could not leave his post because he was assigned to guard the Prime Minister. Mrs. Ben-Gurion replied, "Nonsense! You go to the store—I'll guard the Prime Minister."[110]

• Marvel Comics maven Stan Lee once met Hillary Clinton; he introduced his wife, Joanie, to her as his trophy wife. (Hillary smiled.) A couple of weeks later, he and Joanie met Hillary again at a party. Since he wasn't sure if she would remember them, he started to make a re-introduction, but Hillary said, "Hello, Stan. How are you and your trophy wife?"[111]

• Eleanor Roosevelt was concerned about the problems of low-paid workers. The First Lady occasionally invited low-paid workers to dinner in the White House, where she made sure they sat by her husband, President Franklin Delano Roosevelt. That way, the low-paid workers could talk to the President about their problems.[112]

Justice

• A king put on trial a man who had stolen bread because he was starving. The king found the man guilty and ordered him to be hung.

On his way to the gallows, the thief said that before he was hung, he would like to teach the king how to perform the miracle of planting a pomegranate and having it grow to maturity overnight. The king was willing to learn how to perform the miracle, so the thief dug a hole in the ground, took a pomegranate seed out of his pocket, and said, "Now a man who has never taken anything that did not belong to him must plant this seed. Because I am a thief, I cannot do it." However, none of the king's court was able to plant the seed, each of them admitting that at some time he had taken something that did not belong to him; in fact, even the king was not able to plant the seed. Therefore, the man who had stolen bread because he was starving said, "You are all mighty and powerful and want nothing, and yet you cannot plant the seed while I who have stolen bread because I was starving am to be hanged." The king pardoned the thief.[113]

• How important is politics? The ancient Chinese scholar and teacher Confucius once heard a woman crying in a remote area he was traveling through, and he asked her why she was crying. She replied that she was crying because tigers had killed both her father and her son. He asked why she didn't move to an area where wild animals posed less danger. The woman stated that she stayed because the local ruler was just in his dealings with the people. Hearing that, Confucius turned to his students and told them, "My children, remember this—oppressive government is fiercer than a tiger."[114]

Language

• While trading with the Native Americans, members of the 1804-1806 Lewis and Clark expedition sometimes found language to be a major but not insurmountable barrier. During one trading session, Native American chief Cameahwait spoke Shoshone to Sacagawea, his sister who served as guide to Meriwether Lewis and William Clark. Sacagawea then spoke in Hidatsa to her husband, Toussaint Charbonneau, who then spoke in French to expedition member

Francis Labiche, who then spoke in English to Lewis and Clark. Despite the language barrier, the trading was successful.[115]

• When John Adams was in London and his wife, Abigail, was back home in the United States, she wrote him, worried about the cold weather, and advised him to keep warm. He wrote back, saying that if it were cold at night, he would take a virgin to bed to keep him warm. (Mr. Adams then explained that in the British slang of the time, a "virgin" was a hot-water bottle.)[116]

Lawyers

• As an African-American lawyer fighting racism in the deep South, Thurgood Marshall witnessed and suffered much prejudice. At one southern town, he showed up to defend a black client and learned that his client had been lynched. In another southern town, the sheriff told Mr. Marshall, "The sun never set on a n*gger on this town." By sunset, Mr. Marshall made sure that he was sitting on a train heading north. Once, he vigorously defended George Crawford, a black man who was accused of murdering a maid and the maid's white employer. At the end of the trial, Mr. Crawford was sentenced to life in prison. Mr. Marshall felt that this was evidence that the state's case was weak, since blacks accused of murdering whites were almost always sentenced to death. Mr. Marshall asked Mr. Crawford if he wanted a new trial, and Mr. Crawford asked if the jurors in the new trial could find him guilty and sentence him to death. On hearing that they could, Mr. Crawford said, "Tell them the defense rests."[117]

• When Abraham Lincoln was a lawyer, he was opposed by a big-city lawyer who wore a then-fashionable shirt that buttoned up the back. The case was being tried in the country, and Mr. Lincoln knew that big-city fashions wouldn't go over well there, so he waited until it grew hot and his opponent took off his coat and vest, then he addressed the jury, "Gentleman of the jury, having justice on my side, I don't think you will be at all influenced by the gentleman's pretended knowledge of the law, when you see he does not even know which side of his shirt should be in front."[118]

Letters

• During the Revolutionary War, John Adams went to Paris to represent the new United States to the French government. Separated from his wife, Abigail, he wrote her many, many letters. However, the tone of the letters was formal and cold, unlike the warm, affectionate letters he had sent her while they were separated in the United States. Why the formal, cold tone? Mr. Adams was afraid that enemy warships would intercept American or French ships carrying his letters, and that the enemy would ridicule the letters. Despite this reason for the formal, cold tone of the letters, Mr. Adams had made a big mistake, and his wife let him know it in no uncertain terms. She wrote him, "By heaven, ... you have changed hearts with some frozen Laplander, or made a voyage to a region that has chilled every drop of your blood. The affection I feel for my friend [a term Abigail called her husband] is of the tenderest kind. Angels can witness to its purity—what care I then for the ridicule of Britain should this testimony of it fall into its hands?" Mr. Adams' letters to his wife quickly regained their usual warm, affectionate tone.[119]

• Just after the existence of Richard Nixon's secret tapes had been discovered and the Supreme Court had ordered that they be given to a special prosecutor, science fiction writer Philip K. Dick received this fortune in a Chinese restaurant: "DEEDS DONE IN SECRET HAVE A WAY OF BECOMING FOUND OUT." Mr. Dick sent the fortune to the White House, writing, "I think a mistake has been made; by accident I got Mr. Nixon's fortune. Does he have mine?" He received no answer from the White House.[120]

Mishaps

• In 1969, the town of Picoaza, Ecuador, elected as its mayor a foot powder named Pulvapies. This is what happened. Taking advantage of an upcoming election, the Pulvapies foot powder company rolled out an advertising campaign that made it seem as if their foot powder was a real person who was really running for mayor. The ads proclaimed in big letters: VOTE FOR PULVAPIES. Of course, a foot powder cannot become mayor, so the election was voided, a new election was held, and a real human being was elected mayor. However, the new mayor made himself unpopular, and these signs appeared in the town of Picoaza: "BRING BACK PULVAPIES!" and "PULVAPIES, THE BEST MAYOR WE EVER HAD!"[121]

• Sir Rudolf Bing, general manager of the Metropolitan Opera, once committed a faux pas when the wife of President Lyndon Johnson attended a performance in his box. Her armchair was seated in the second row, and when she stood up to acknowledge the applause at her entrance, he told her that he was moving her chair, and proceeded to move it to the first row. Unfortunately, just as he could not understand her Texas accent, she could not understand his Austrian accent—and so she sat on nothing and fell down in front of 4,000 people. (She was gracious about the accident, but the Secret Service was not.)[122]

• Actress Shelly Winters could be very outspoken. At a Chicago Film Festival, she met Mayor Richard Daley. Amazed at how young he looked, she was positive that he had had plastic surgery done. Therefore, she commented, "You look great. You haven't aged a day since I met you 20 years ago. Who does your work?" Of course, she was unaware that 20 years ago she had met then-Mayor Richard *J.* Daley, and she was now talking to his son: Richard *M.* Daley.[123]

• As a youth, Marvel Comics maven Stan Lee worked in a movie house on Broadway. Once, first lady Eleanor Roosevelt visited the theater, and Mr. Lee had the privilege of showing her to her seat. He walked down the aisle with his head held high, and he tripped over the leg of a patron and fell. Mrs. Roosevelt put her hands on his shoulders and asked if he was all right. (He was fine—except for his pride.)[124]

• In August of 1806, while returning from exploring the Louisiana Purchase and the American West, Meriwether Lewis went hunting with Pierre Cruzatte. Big mistake. One of Mr. Cruzatte's eyes was blind and his other eye was nearsighted. He saw Mr. Lewis, thought he was an elk, and shot him in a buttock. Mr. Lewis spent most of the rest of the journey home lying on his stomach.[125]

Money

• Manuel Candamo was a President of Peru before World War II. Sometimes his children would come into his study while he was working, and he would tell them, "My dears, I am busy. Just play quietly on the floor. Build walls and castles with all the pretty bricks in those boxes." Several boxes were in the study, all of which were filled with gold coins. His children used to build entire cities with the coins. (Later, Mr. Candamo was assassinated. His children went to Paris, where his young son waited in line to see a bank clerk, who told him that he was busy. But when the clerk read the letter the boy presented to him, his demeanor immediately changed. The clerk took the letter to a bank VIP, who came over to the boy and said, "Well, my boy, how much money do you want? We will keep this letter for you while you are in Paris. It is an open letter of credit, drawn upon the Bank of England. I have never seen one before!")[126]

• Satirist Michael Moore, the director of *Roger and Me*, wanted to find out in the last Presidential election how greedy politicians were for money, so he went to the Alternatives Federal Credit Union in Ithaca, New York, and set up several checking accounts, then sent checks for $75 or $100 to the leading Presidential candidates and Ross Perot. The checks were from organizations Mr. Moore had created for this purpose, including Pedophiles for Free Trade, Abortionists for Buchanan, and Hemp Growers of America. Many of the checks were cashed; however, the Bob Dole campaign returned two checks from Satan Worshippers for Dole, and H. Ross Perot returned a check from the John Wayne Gacy Fan Club.[127]

• Jim Wright, a Democrat and former Speaker of the U.S. House of Representatives, tells a story about then-Speaker Sam Rayburn trying to raise money for Adlai Stevenson's presidential campaign in 1952. A man came to him with a list of names of big Texas millionaires and said, "I've talked to them, and each will give. But they say you'll have to call and ask them, Mr. Speaker." Mr. Rayburn looked at the list, then said, "I've done something in the past for every one of these people. Now they want me obligated to them. I haven't been, and I won't be!" Then Mr. Rayburn threw away the list of names.[128]

• Judge Roy Bean, the Law West of the Pecos, liked to make money and he didn't mind using his position as Judge to make it. For example, when he fined someone, the fine went into his own pocket. Once, a man died after being blown by a strong wind off a bridge. In his capacity as coroner, Judge Bean examined the body and discovered $40 and a concealed pistol. In his capacity as judge, he fined the dead man $40 for carrying a concealed pistol and put the money in his own pocket—he also kept the pistol.[129]

• Ralph Nader's father, Nathra, was amused when Ronald Reagan ranted about "Welfare queens" during the 1980 Presidential campaign. Nathra pointed out, correctly, "When the rich take our tax money, it's called a subsidy. When the poor get it, it's called Welfare. Actually, the rich are our biggest Welfare cases." Nathra was known for discussing politics in his restaurant. His customers said, "At Nader's place, for a nickel you got a cup of coffee and 10 minutes of conversation."[130]

• Unfunded mandates are nothing new. In the old West, according to Don Hampton Biggers, the Texas legislature once passed a bounty law, ordering local governments to pay $1 for 12 jack rabbits or 12 prairie dogs, $1 per coyote wolf scalp, and $5 per lobo scalp. To avoid going bankrupt, many counties ignored the law, and the Texas legislature, realizing that it had made a mistake, quickly repealed the law.[131]

• In the National Archives in Washington, D.C., is a letter from a 12-year-old Fidel Castro to President Franklin Delano Roosevelt: "My good friend Roosvelt. I don't know very English, but I know as much as I write to you. If you like, give me a ten dollars bill green American in the letter because never I have not seen a ten dollars bill green American and I would like to have one of them."[132]

• Marianne Williamson has written about world hunger. Occasionally, someone will tell her that they are very depressed because of world hunger. She then asks the person, "Do you give five dollars a week to one of the organizations that feed the hungry?" Ms. Williamson has noticed that the people who are trying to help solve the problems of the world are happier than those who aren't.[133]

• Mr. Justice Hawkins (1817-1907) once received a brief. After six weeks had gone by, his clerk wrote the man who had prepared the brief. In his letter, the clerk stated that a cheque should be sent immediately to Mr. Hawkins. The solicitor who had prepared the brief wrote back, saying, "If Mr. Hawkins had taken the trouble to open the brief, he would have found the cheque inside."[134]

• Hetty Green was known as the Witch of Wall Street, and she was a miser, as was her father. In fact, her father once turned down the gift of an expensive cigar because he was afraid that he would like it so much that he would start buying and smoking expensive cigars and stop buying the inexpensive cigars that he always smoked.[135]

• Lady Nancy Astor once canvassed a town on the seashore for votes in the company of an officer of Her Majesty's Navy. A small child opened one door she knocked on. Lady Astor said, "Is your mother at home?" The child replied, "No, but she said if a lady comes in with a sailor, they're to use the upstairs room and leave 10 bob."[136]

• Most of us consider J.P. Morgan to have been a rich man; after all, he died in 1913 with an estate worth $68 million, not counting his art masterpieces. However, when industrialist Andrew Carnegie (a super-rich man) heard about Mr. Morgan's net worth at his death, he said, "And to think he was not a rich man."[137]

• Demonax the Cynic philosopher once ran across a magician who was selling tokens that would make people give the token owner anything he wanted. Demonax said, "I've already got one." Then he took the magician into a shop, gave the shop owner a piece of money, and said, "Give me a loaf of bread."[138]

• After Calvin Coolidge was married, his wife bought a book titled *Our Family Physician* for $8—a large amount of money at the time. Mr. Coolidge never spoke about the purchase, but one day his wife looked inside the cover and saw that he had written, "Don't see any recipe for curing suckers."[139]

• A friend of lesbian humorist Ellen Orleans wants everyone to know the financial impact that gays have, so he stamps "Gay Money Gay Money Gay Money" on all of his paper money before he spends it.[140]

Names

• When Herbert Hoover worked for President Calvin Coolidge as Secretary of Commerce, he warned him about an impending financial crisis. However, when he was elected President, he did nothing to stem the crisis he felt was coming—big business had donated heavily to his campaign, and big business didn't want him to interfere with the economy. Because Mr. Hoover was President when the Great Depression started, and because he was the man in charge, he bore the blame. Hungry men traveling in hopes of finding work or at least food gathered together in shantytowns called "Hoovervilles." To keep warm, they used newspapers, which they called "Hoover blankets." A pants pocket turned inside out to show that it was empty was a "Hoover flag." A broken-down car pulled by a mule was known as a "Hoover wagon." The widely despised President Hoover traveled throughout the United States, and everywhere he saw signs saying, "In Hoover we trusted—now we are busted." In West Virginia, when he was given a 21-gun salute, someone complained, "By gum, they missed him." President Hoover was so unpopular that a joke stated that he had asked someone for a nickel so he could treat a friend to a soda. Instead of a nickel, he received a dime and the comment, "Treat all of them."[141]

• Henry Brown wanted to escape from slavery and become a free man, so he hid inside a wooden crate that was being mailed from Virginia to Philadelphia, Pennsylvania. Although he spent part of the journey upside down, he was happy to be a free man once the crate was opened in Philadelphia. From then on, friends and acquaintances called him "Box" Brown.[142]

• When Dennis Banks and other Native Americans were thinking of a name for their new activist organization advocating the civil rights of Native Americans, someone suggested Concerned Indian Americans. However, they didn't want their organization to be known as CIA, so they adopted the name American Indian Movement, or AIM.[143]

• Although the citizens of France were burdened by high taxes, Marie Antoinette continued to spend vast amounts of money. Once, she decided to have a simple wardrobe, but some of her straw hats cost more than an average working man made in a year! Because of her extravagance, the French people started to call her "Madame Deficit."[144]

• "Break" dancing got its name in New York in 1969 when disc jockey Afrika Bambaataa suggested that gang members take a break from fighting and killing each other and instead express their rivalry by competing in dancing.[145]

• United States Congressman Brooks Hays was once presented to Pope John XXIII. "I'm a Baptist," said Mr. Hays. "I'm John," replied the Holy Father.[146]

Nobel Peace Prize

• Opposing the rich landowners and the soldiers who supported them in Guatemala in 1980 could be dangerous. Rigoberta Menchú organized cotton and sugar plantation workers in preparation for a strike to demand better working conditions and higher pay. Soon, soldiers started looking for her. At one point, while being chased by soldiers, she ducked into a crowded church, let her hair down, and joined the other people kneeling at their prayers. Fortunately, the ruse worked, and she was not captured. In 1992, she won the Nobel Peace Prize for her work helping Mayan workers in Guatemala. With the money she won with the Nobel Peace Prize, she set up the Vicente Manchú Foundation to promote human rights in Guatemala. The foundation is named after her father, who died trying to help workers in Guatemala.[147]

• While he was at the United Nations, Ralph Bunche worked tirelessly to bring about peace between Jews and Arabs (at least temporarily). On the island of Rhodes in Greece, he succeeded, and he then gave the Jewish and the Arab contingents gifts of beautiful pottery on which appeared the words "Rhodes Armistice Negotiations." The contingents asked him what he would have done with the pottery if he had not been able to bring about peace. Dr. Bunche joked, "If no agreement had been reached, I would have smashed this pottery over your heads." In 1950, Dr. Bunche won the Nobel Peace Prize.[148]

Photography

• When famed Canadian portrait photographer Yousuf Karsh took a photograph of Winston Churchill to be added to the Canadian National Archives, he had only two minutes to take the photograph because the British Prime Minister was busy leading wartime Britain. The portrait became famous, and it made Mr. Karsh famous. Of course, Mr. Karsh had the lights set up in advance, but he had to get exactly the right pose from Prime Minister Churchill in the two minutes allotted for one shot—and Prime Minister Churchill meant ONLY one shot. Mr. Karsh decided that he wanted a photograph of Churchill without a cigar because a man like Churchill didn't need a prop, so Mr. Karsh showed Churchill an ashtray. Churchill simply waved away the ashtray, but Mr. Karsh reached up and removed the cigar from Churchill's mouth, then as quickly as possible took his photograph. The photograph captured Churchill as he was at the time: steely, without humor, and utterly determined—the perfect leader for wartime

Britain. (Later, Mr. Karsh took a photograph of the Rt. Hon. Sir Richard Stafford Cripps, who held a lighted cigarette behind his back, saying that he was taking no chances because he had heard what had happened to Churchill's cigar. In addition, American Secretary of War Henry Lewis Stimson asked Mr. Karsh for permission to smoke during a portrait-taking session. After getting permission, he said, "I didn't want to take any chances after what I've heard you did to Churchill.")[149]

• Chuck Close took photographs of President Bill Clinton during a photo session in which he learned something about the former President that most people don't know—that in at least one way, he is sensitive about his appearance. When Mr. Close showed up for the photo session, Mr. Clinton said, "D*mn, look at those bags under my eyes. I forgot to take my water pills." The water pills help to reduce the size of the bags under a person's eyes, and evidently Mr. Clinton was sensitive about the bags under his eyes.[150]

Chapter 4: From Prayer to Public Speaking

Prayer

• Rufus Jones and some Quakers journeyed to Nazi Germany in 1938 and went into Gestapo headquarters in an attempt to be allowed to extend relief to Jews. After speaking with "Hangman" Hydrick, the Quakers were left alone in a room, and they bowed their heads silently in prayer in the only Quaker meeting ever to be held at Gestapo headquarters. The Nazis soon returned, and one of the Nazis remarked that the room had been bugged and any word that had been spoken had been recorded. Mr. Jones wrote later, "We were glad then that we had kept the period of quiet."[151]

• The father of Joan Ryan, a columnist for the *San Francisco Chronicle*, is a die-hard Republican, but even he had a hard time stomaching George W. Bush and the massive debt he and the neocons ran up on the national credit card. On Thanksgiving of 2005, Joan and her father were talking on the telephone when he said that he had to hang up because he was going to Mass. Joan asked him if he would pray for President Bush to become wise. He replied, "I believe in the power of prayer, but it can only do so much."[152]

Prejudice

• Many people who have contracted HIV or AIDS have been discriminated against. Ryan White, a teenager in Kokomo, Indiana, contracted HIV through a blood transfusion that he needed because he was a hemophiliac. School officials and many parents did not want Ryan to go to their school, and many people protested against Ryan in the streets. When Ryan ate in a restaurant, the proprietors of the restaurant threw away the dishes and silverware Ryan had used. Once, someone shot a bullet into his home. Ryan and his family were forced to move to Cicero, Illinois, before he died of AIDS in 1990. Richard,

Robert, and Randy Ray also contracted HIV because of blood transfusions that were needed because they were hemophiliacs. After a firebomb destroyed their home in Arcadia, Florida, they and their family moved away. Actor Paul Michael Glaser's wife, Elizabeth, contracted the HIV virus during childbirth when she was given a blood transfusion. She didn't know that she had HIV and passed the virus on to two of her children. After people learned that the Glaser's four-year-old daughter, April, had developed AIDS, they didn't want their children to go to school or play with her. April died when she was seven years old. Fortunately, today we can test for HIV and AIDS in blood, so these diseases are no longer contracted through receiving a blood transfusion.[153]

• The great black dancer Bill Robinson, aka Mr. Bojangles, fought prejudice. In Dallas, Texas, to perform at a benefit, he asked if a few black friends could be in the audience next to his wife. This was a very unusual request in those days, but his request was granted. A couple of days later, the Robinsons wanted to get to New York quickly to see Joe Louis fight. To get back in time for the fight, they would have to ride the all-white train, so he asked for permission to ride the train. Again, this was an unusual request, but it was granted. On the train, people learned that the famous Mr. Bojangles was on the train, so they and their children kept going to his car to see him. For hours, Mr. Bojangles put on a free show. A few weeks after this (and as a result of white people being impressed with the behavior of Mr. Bojangles and his wife), the Robinsons learned that for the first time ever, some black police officers were being hired to work in the black sections of Dallas—social progress that was made possible by Mr. Bojangles simply acting as a human being worthy of respect and dignity (and treating fans really well).[154]

• During the Civil Rights movement, Freedom Riders headed south. Laws had been passed outlawing segregation on public transportation, but in some places segregation continued. Therefore, the Freedom Riders, who were both white and black, rode on buses throughout the south to test whether public transportation had really been desegregated. In Birmingham, Alabama, the Freedom Fighters were assaulted, and James Person, who was black, and James Peck, who was white, were brutally beaten—Mr. Peck ended up with 53 stitches in his face. Outside Anniston, Alabama, a bus was fire bombed as a mob broke windows and punctured tires. In Montgomery, Alabama, the Freedom Riders were attacked by a mob, and James Zwerg, a white student, and John Seigenthaler, John F. Kennedy's representative, were beaten until they were unconscious. A reporter asked Police Commissioner L.B. Sullivan if he had sent for ambulances, but the police commissioner replied, "Every white ambulance [business] in town reports their vehicles have broken down."[155]

• Once, Sojourner Truth and her friend Laura Haviland were traveling together. Ms. Truth was an African-American woman, and Ms. Haviland was a wealthy white woman. A streetcar stopped for the two women, and Ms. Truth tried to board the streetcar first. However, the streetcar conductor pushed Ms. Truth away and told her to let the lady get on first. Ms. Truth replied, "I am a lady, too," and attempted to board the streetcar again. The conductor stopped Ms. Truth and asked Ms. Haviland if she was Ms. Truth's owner. Ms. Haviland replied, "No—she belongs to humanity." Again, the conductor pushed Ms. Truth away, this time with such force that he dislocated her shoulder. The two women stopped trying to board the streetcar, but they recorded the number of the streetcar and reported the brutality of the conductor. He was arrested for assault and battery, and he lost his job.[156]

• Texas State Comptroller Bob Bullock knew everyone, good and bad, in politics. At a political shindig where all kinds were invited, he was standing with Ann Richards and Molly Ivins and with Charles Miles, who was in charge of Mr. Bullock's personnel department. A racist judge greeted Mr. Bullock, met Ms. Ivins, and then was introduced to Mr. Miles, who is African-American. The racist judge was not happy, but he shook Mr. Miles' hand—barely. Then the racist judge asked about Ms. Richards, "And who is this lovely lady?" Ms. Richards, knowing the judge was racist, grinned widely and replied, "I am Mrs. Miles." (Actually, her husband was David Richards, but they divorced.)[157]

• African-American Arthur Ashe faced prejudice despite being a tennis star and Wimbledon champion. Most of the time, he kept his composure, but early in his career, he once asked a racist, "What do you want me to do, paint myself with whitewash?" In 1983, he became HIV-positive as a result of a blood transfusion. When he went public with the news that he had AIDS, a reporter asked him if having AIDS was his biggest burden. Mr. Ashe replied, "No ... being black is the greatest burden I've had to bear. Having to live as a minority in America. Even now it continues to feel like an extra weight tied around me."[158]

• Barbara Jordan was the first African-American woman in the Texas Senate, where she became famous for her oratory. According to author and syndicated columnist Molly Ivins, people used to bring their racist friends to the Texas Senate when Ms. Jordan was scheduled to talk. The racist friend would be shocked and ask, "Who is that n*gger?" And then the racist friend would be even more shocked as oratory worthy of Abraham Lincoln poured from Ms. Jordan's lips. For example, she once orated, "My faith in the Con-sti-tu-tion is whole; it is com-plete; it is to-tal."[159]

• The first African American to be appointed to the United States Supreme Court was Thurgood Marshall. His father had endured much prejudice, but he always responded to it with dignity. Once, he was working as a butler in the home of a wealthy white widow. At a party, the woman said to her pet poodle, "Show the people which you would rather be—a n*gger or dead." As the poodle had been trained to do, it rolled over on its back and held its legs in the air. Thurgood's father witnessed the scene, then he left by the front door and never returned.[160]

• In 1971, Coca-Cola produced a TV commercial promoting love, peace, and Coca-Cola. In this commercial, people from many countries and of both sexes and all races sang, "I'd like to teach the world to sing in perfect harmony. I'd like to buy the world a Coke and keep it company. I'd like to see the world for once all standing hand in hand and hear them echo through the hills for peace throughout the land." South Africa asked that a version of this TV commercial be made in which no blacks would appear—it didn't get it.[161]

• Monte Irvin was one of the first African-American athletes to play major-league baseball in the 20th century. In Orange, New Jersey, Mr. Irvin wanted to buy property on which he could build a house, but he was unable to because of the color of his skin. Therefore, he proposed to his lawyer that the lawyer buy the property and then Mr. Irvin would buy the property from him. Unfortunately, the lawyer responded, "No, I'm afraid of that, and I'm president of the Republican Club." Mr. Irwin got a new lawyer—a Democrat.[162]

• During the days of segregation, Martin Luther King, Sr., took his son to buy shoes. Inside a shoe store, they sat down in the chairs near the door, but an angry clerk told them, "What do you think you're doing? You know you can't sit there." King, Sr., replied, "I see nothing wrong with these seats." The clerk shouted, "The colored sit in the back." King, Sr., responded, "We'll buy shoes sitting here, or we won't buy shoes at all." Eventually, the Kings left without buying shoes.[163]

• In 1929, First Lady Lou Hoover invited the wife of a black Congressperson to come to the White House. This made a lot of people angry, and the Texas legislature even proposed impeaching President Herbert Hoover. The President told the First Lady, "Don't worry, Lou. One of the consolations of orthodox religion is that it provides a hot Hell for the Texas legislature."[164]

• In 1996, a high school principal in Alabama set a policy that interracial couples could not attend the school prom. When a biracial student asked him why he had set the policy, he replied that he wanted to prevent "mistakes" such as her. This story has a happy ending. The principal was fired, and biracial couples had a good time at the prom.[165]

• After George W. Bush was elected to the Presidency of the United States by the Supreme Court in the 2000 election, feminist comedian Kate Clinton ranted to an African-American friend about how powerless and disenfranchised she felt. The African-American friend gave her a look that said plainly, "How do you like it?"[166]

• Actor Cesar Romero hated application forms that asked people if they were Hispanic or white. He wondered whether the people who create these forms had ever seen a Hispanic person.[167]

Presidents

• In 1903, union organizer Mother Jones led a group of child laborers from Philadelphia mills to New York City in a march designed to bring attention to the existence of child labor in the United States and to improve the lives of the working children. She even attempted to meet with President Theodore Roosevelt and have him see the mill children, but he resisted her attempts, saying that he believed in states' rights and therefore child labor was the concern of states, not of the United States. Years later, Mother Jones said of President Roosevelt, "He had a lot of secret service men watching an old woman and an army of children. You fellows do elect wonderful Presidents."[168]

• President Jimmy Carter and some members of the media once visited a village in India where the most important energy source was a huge pit filled with cow manure. The methane gas rising from the pit was used to light the lamps in the village. Surveying the stinky pit, Sam Donaldson joked, "If I fell in, you'd pull me out, wouldn't you, Mr. President?" President Carter may have been thinking about the rough time Mr. Donaldson and the media had been giving him, because he replied, "Certainly—after a suitable interval."[169]

• Realistic moving automatons of the Presidents can be seen at Disneyland and at Disney World. Unfortunately, these cause confusion in the minds of very young students. Once, a teacher told her elementary school students, "We still remember Mr. Lincoln, although he has been dead for over a hundred years." One of her students objected: "Oh, he's not dead. He's alive! I saw him at Disneyland."[170]

• A man once took his small daughter to meet Abraham Lincoln, and told her not to mind President Lincoln's ugly face because he was a kind man. The child sat on the President's lap and was charmed by the way President Lincoln spoke to her. Turning to her father, she said, "But, father, his face isn't ugly at all. I think he's beautiful."[171]

• A friend once bet Will Rogers that he couldn't make President Calvin Coolidge, who was normally very tight-lipped, laugh. Will accepted the bet, and when he was introduced to the President, he said, "I'm sorry. I didn't get the name." President Coolidge laughed.[172]

Problem-Solving

• In Greensburg, Pennsylvania, police arrested several women—the wives of striking miners—who had gathered to shout abuse at strikebreakers, aka scabs. The judge sentenced each woman to pay a fine of $30 or go to jail for 30 days. Since $30 was more than a miner made in a month, the women went to jail—and their nursing babies went to jail with them. Fortunately, union organizer Mother Jones had a plan. She told the women to sing constantly and to sing loudly. For five days, the women did exactly that. Complaints from neighbors poured in, and when the judge told Mother Jones to make the women stop singing, she declined, pointing out that there was nothing wrong in women singing patriotic songs and mothers singing lullabies to their children. After five days of constant noise from the women and constant complaints from the neighbors, the judge could stand it no longer and let the women go free.[173]

• George Armstrong Custer was a problem-solver. On the banks of the Chickahominy River, he once listened for a while to his superior officers argue about the depth of the river, then he rode his horse into the river and determined exactly how deep the river was. He was also headstrong. He employed several Native American scouts before the Battle of the Little Bighorn. They advised him not to fight the Sioux because the Sioux outnumbered them, but he insisted on starting the battle. One of the Crow scouts then put on Native American clothing. When Mr. Custer asked the Crow scout why he had done that, the scout replied, "We are all going to die today, so I intend to meet the Great Spirit dressed as an Indian, not as a white man." Mr. Custer was so angry that he fired all of the Native American scouts, and so none of them died in the battle.[174]

• Rabbis are concerned with justice, even when a particular Jew is not just. A Christian once lent money to a Jew, with God and the tree they were under serving as witnesses. Later, the Jew refused to pay back the money, saying that he had not borrowed any money from the Christian at all. Rabbi Hariri heard the case, and he whispered something into the ear of the Christian, who then went away and did not return. Becoming impatient, the Jew asked where the Christian had gone. Rabbi Hariri answered, "I have sent him to bring a branch from that tree, under which he lent you the money." "Oh," the Jew said, "he will not be back until the evening." Rabbi Hariri then told the Jew, "When the Christian returns, pay him the money you owe him. The tree has borne witness."[175]

• In the days of slavery, African-Americans had few ways of helping each other. Baumfree, a slave in Hurley, New York, discovered that Isabella, his young daughter, had become the property of a harsh master named John Nealy who beat her. Once, he had beaten her with a rod that was very hot, and the rod scarred her for life. As a slave, Baumfree was unable to get protection for her from the law courts. However, he did what he could do. He found another slave owner who did not beat his slaves, and he convinced him to buy his daughter. Later, as a free woman, Isabella became famous as an abolitionist and women's rights activist under the name Sojourner Truth.[176]

• During the Roman civil wars when Julius Caesar was fighting against Sextus Pompey for power, Caesar landed on the coast of North Africa. As he jumped from his ship into the shallow water, he stumbled and fell. Knowing that his superstitious Roman troops would regard his stumbling as an unlucky omen, Caesar decided to make his troops think he had fallen on purpose. He grabbed two fistfuls of sand, stood up, and raised his hands so his troops could see the sand. He then yelled, "AFRICA, I HOLD YOU IN MY HANDS!" Hearing these inspiring words, his troops charged upon the beach with high morale.[177]

• In 1974, the citizens of Coacaloco, a small town in Mexico, decided that they needed a new mayor because their current mayor was corrupt and kept stealing the profits from the sales of the bananas they grew. Four thousand citizens stormed the mayor's residence and found the mayor, Señor José Ramon del Cuet, hiding under a desk. They pulled him out and demanded that he resign. He refused, so the citizens brought in a box of bananas and forced him to begin eating them. After being forced to eat 12 pounds of bananas, Señor Cuet decided to resign as mayor.[178]

• Graça Simbine Machel wanted her native country, Mozambique, to be free of Portuguese rule, so she met with other leaders of the group called FRELIMO to figure out how to accomplish their goal. FRELIMO's members had to be very careful not to get caught plotting the overthrow of the government; therefore, they pretended to have parties at Lisbon University and played music very loudly. However, instead of partying, everyone was discussing politics.[179]

• Eleanor Roosevelt stood up for women, including women journalists. Lorena Hickok, an Associated Press reporter, told her that one way she could help women reporters would be to hold a weekly press conference at which only women reporters could be present. Ms. Roosevelt accepted the suggestion, and soon the major media of the day hired women reporters so they could have someone present at those press conferences.[180]

• In 1958, President Dwight D. Eisenhower threw out an autographed baseball at the season opener of the Senators and the Red Sox. All of the players, hoping to get a baseball autographed by the President, ran after it—except for the Red Sox' Jimmy Piersall, who walked over to President Eisenhower, handed him a baseball and a pen, and asked for his autograph. Mr. Piersall explained later, "I never did like crowds."[181]

• Judge Roy Bean, the Law West of the Pecos, did not like it when one of his decisions was questioned. One day, a lawyer questioned one of his decisions, so Judge Bean turned to a Texas Ranger and asked what he would do if the court ordered that the lawyer be taken out and hanged. The Texas Ranger replied, "I'd take him out and hang him." Thereafter, the lawyer did not question any of Judge Bean's rulings.[182]

• Juan Peron, dictator of Argentina, was a very intelligent man. He once gave his wife, Eva, a 1952 Rolls Royce that was bulletproofed in such a way that the passengers—but not the driver—would be protected. Mr. Peron reasoned that if the driver were not protected from flying bullets then the driver would not accept a bribe to drive the car into an ambush.[183]

• J.P. Morgan was a master negotiator. When he wanted a group of recalcitrant leaders to come to an agreement, he used to invite them on his yacht, then refuse to let the yacht go into harbor until the leaders had come to an agreement. Another tactic was to lock leaders in his library and refuse to open the doors until the leaders had come to an agreement.[184]

• Most able-bodied young men were forced to serve in the army of Czar Nicholas before the Russian Revolution, but some men found ways to keep out of the army. To avoid conscription, Isaac Abramson cut the tendons of his toes so that he limped when he walked.[185]

Public Speaking

• Ohio governor Jim Rhodes once gave a speech at the dedication of a building on the Ohio University campus in Portsmouth, Ohio. Unfortunately, before he spoke, many other people spoke, including the mayor, the head of the labor union, the state representative, and the chair of the city council. Therefore, when Governor Rhodes was finally able to speak, he told this story: An agricultural pest was threatening Ohio crops, so state troopers were under orders to stop every farm vehicle that came along. Troopers stopped a farmer and asked what he had in his truck. The farmer answered, "A load of manure, and John, my son." A little further down the road, troopers again stopped the farmer and asked what he had in the truck. Again, the farmer replied, "A load of manure, and John, my son." The third time troopers stopped the truck and received the answer, "A load of manure, and John, my son," John looked up at his father and requested, "Next time, introduce me first."[186]

• Educator Alice Trillin once listened to a speech by New York governor George Pataki in which he spoke about his older brother, who grew up in a home with modest financial resources but was accepted to Yale. Their post office worker father drove to New Haven, Connecticut, to ask the Yale director of admissions how the son of a postal worker could be expected to go to Yale without a scholarship. (The director of admissions immediately called the Yale Westchester Alumni Association to find a solution to that particular problem.) After governor Pataki had finished the speech, Ms. Trillin told him, "That was one of the best speeches I've ever heard. Why in the world are you a Republican?"[187]

• In 2007, when John McCain was running for the office of President of the United States, a man told him after hearing a luncheon speech, "I've seen in the press where in your run for the presidency, you've been sucking up to the religious right. I was just wondering how soon do you predict a Republican candidate for President will start sucking up to the old Rockefeller wing of the Republican Party?" Mr. McCain hesitated, then replied, "I'm probably going to get in trouble, but what's wrong with sucking up to everybody?"[188]

• President Lyndon Johnson was a plainspoken man who knew that American citizens are not especially erudite. When his speech writers sent him a high-falutin' speech complete with quotations from Aristotle, he snorted, "Aristotle! Those folks don't know who the hell Aristotle is!" Therefore, to make the speech more palatable to Americans, whenever President Johnson was supposed to say, "As Aristotle said …," he instead said, "As my dear old pappy used to say …."[189]

• F.E. Smith, later Lord Birkenhead (1872-1930) once asked late in the afternoon that a case of his be postponed because he had been speaking all day in another case, and he was exhausted. The judge granted his request and called another case. However, counsel for this case also asked that his case be postponed. When the judge asked why, the counsel replied, "May it please you, my lord, I, too, am in a state of exhaustion, for I have been listening all day to Mr. Smith."[190]

• Aviator Amelia Earhart spoke her mind. Addressing the Daughters of the American Revolution, she told them, "You really shouldn't have invited me here. I always say what I think, and you may not like it." She then gave her thoughts about war: "You glorify it. You applaud the marching feet and the band and you cheer on the military machine. You really all ought to be drafted." Applause was slight.[191]

• Senator Robert Byrd (D-West Virginia) was a learned man. He once heard a member of Parliament lamenting that Americans were ignorant about English history. Therefore, at a dinner attended by the MP that night, Senator Byrd gave a speech that lasted over an hour and mentioned every king and queen that England had ever had. The speech included the dates of each of their reigns—and the names of each of their consorts.[192]

• Winston Churchill, a politician and a Noble Prize winner in literature, wrote his own speeches. President Franklin Delano Roosevelt listened to a radio broadcast of a speech by Prime Minister Churchill while he was working on his own speech with the help of three ghostwriters. President Roosevelt was impressed by Churchill's speech, and one of his ghostwriters, Robert Sherwood, said, "I'm afraid, Mr. President, he rolls his own."[193]

• William Jennings Bryan used to travel the country by train, stopping in towns and cities to make political speeches. In one small town, no platform was available for him to use to make his speech, so he stood on a piece of farm equipment known as a manure spreader. Standing on the manure spreader, Mr. Bryan told the crowd, "This is the first time I have ever made a speech while standing on the Republican platform."[194]

• During a public speech, Susan B. Anthony was interrupted by a clergyman who had a large family. "The Apostle Paul recommends silence in women," the clergyman shouted. "Why don't you mind him?" Ms. Anthony replied, "The Apostle Paul also recommends celibacy in clergymen. Why don't *you* mind him?"[195]

• In 1914, journalist/historian Don Hampton Biggers ran a tongue-in-cheek campaign for office in the Texas legislature. He told the voters, "Don't waste a good man by sending him to Austin. The country needs good men too much. Send me; I'm already ruined." The campaign worked—he was elected.[196]

• Noam Chomsky is so famous as an intellectual that often he has to schedule his speeches years in advance. Sometimes, years in advance, he is asked for the title of his speech. Mr. Chomsky says, "If I am asked for a title, I suggest 'The Current Crisis in the Middle East.' It has yet to fail."[197]

• A Washington toastmaster spent 15 minutes praising Senator Chauncey Depew. On and on came the compliments for Senator Depew and the description of Senator Depew's virtues. Finally, Mrs. Depew leaned toward her husband and said to him loudly, "Hello, God."[198]

Chapter 5: From Religion to Work

Religion

• Huey Long knew how to get people to vote for him by pretending to be devout. He used to tell the voters that on Sundays, when he was a boy, he would get up early, hitch the horse to the wagon, then take his Catholic grandparents to Mass. After Mass was over, he would use the horse and wagon to take his Baptist grandparents to church. The voters liked what he said, and they voted for him. Once, a political boss told Mr. Long that he didn't know that Mr. Long had Catholic grandparents. "Don't be a d*mn fool," Mr. Long replied. "We didn't even have a horse."[199]

• A Soviet Jew applied for a job and filled out an application form in which he stated that he had a brother in Israel. During the interview for the job, he was asked whether he had any relatives outside the motherland. The Jew's answer—"No"—surprised the interviewer, who pointed out that the Jew had stated in the application form that he had a brother living in Israel. The Jew replied, "He's not outside the motherland—I am."[200]

• Texas congressman Bob Eckhardt died in 2001 at the age of 88. He was a liberal who effectively pursued legislation to benefit the people, including African-American people. Someone once told his mother, "Mrs. Eckhardt, your son is just a little too cozy with the Nigras, don't you think?" She replied, "Oh, I'm afraid that's my fault. I raised him to be a Christian."[201]

• Sir Rudolf Bing happened to overhear one of the members of the chorus—an Italian woman—tell her daughter when President John F. Kennedy came into view during a ticker-tape celebration: "Now watch, Kathy. This is President Kennedy, and he is the first Catholic President of the United States." Kathy was surprised, and she asked, "All the others were Jews?"[202]

Royalty

• Ramachandra Pratap Singh is a prince in Dolapur in India, and he will grow up to be a *maharaja*, or king, like his father. One day, the young prince had an annoying dream. He dreamed that he was attempting to ride a bicycle, but no matter how much he pedaled, he didn't go anywhere. A crowd gathered and laughed at him. Eventually, a green-eyed girl in the crowd asked why a prince such as himself wanted to ride a bicycle. When Ramachandra answered that he wanted to have fun, the green-eyed girl said to him, "Didn't you know that princes and kings have every power on earth except one—the right to have fun?" This dream worried Ramachandra—until his father played a joke on him and showed him that kings and princes can have fun.[203]

• The King and Queen of Sweden attended the 1980 Olympic Winter Games in Lake Placid, New York. Trying to get into an ice hockey game featuring the Swedish team, they were stopped by the ticket taker because their tickets were for another game. The King said that the correct tickets were in his car and he asked to be allowed in without the correct tickets: "Could you make an exception for us, please? You see, I'm the King of Sweden." The ticket taker responded, "Sure you are, and I suppose this is the Queen." The King and Queen of Sweden went back to their car to get the correct tickets, only to see it being towed away.[204]

• King Christian X of Denmark was a good person. Although Denmark capitulated quickly when invaded by Germans during World War II, the Danes resisted the Holocaust by removing almost all of Denmark's Jewish citizens to neutral Sweden, where they were safe. Adolf Hitler admired the non-Jewish citizens of Denmark and once suggested to King Christian X that the governments of the two countries be combined into one government. King Christian X replied, "I have given your suggestion much thought. But at my age, I think I am too old to rule over two countries."[205]

• Hanro was a royal minister who fell into disgrace and was exiled during the Chou (aka Zhou) dynasty (ca. 1122-221 B.C.E.). For a long time, Hanro lived as a recluse, until the king recalled him from exile. Hanro mounted a horse and started to return to the royal court, but then he decided that he liked being a recluse better than being a court minister, so he turned his horse around and headed back to his mountain home. However, he rode his horse backwards, so that he could not be said to have turned his back on the king's wishes.[206]

• Many movies have been made about Queen Elizabeth I, the "Virgin Queen" of Great Britain. Of course, people wonder whether she was really a virgin all her life. Asked about this in 1972, actress Glenda Jackson, who acted the role of the queen twice, replied, "Not the way I play her." By the way, British author and historian Alison Weir thinks that yes, Queen Elizabeth I was a virgin all her life. As evidence, she points to Elizabeth's own words: "I do not live in a corner. A thousand eyes see all I do."[207]

• It's important to arrange for quietness in your life. As Japanese emperor, Hirohito was very busy, constantly attending meetings and other functions. One day, he was driven to a place where a meeting was supposed to be held, but no one was there. He walked into the middle of the big open hall, bowed to the quietness, smiled, and then told his advisors, "We must schedule more appointments like this. I haven't enjoyed myself so much in a long time."[208]

• Edward de Vere, a courtier devoted to Queen Elizabeth I, once executed a low and obsequious bow before her majesty—and farted. He was so distressed that he exiled himself from the court for seven years, by which time he thought the fart would have been forgotten. Returning to court, he bowed before Queen Elizabeth I, who told him, "Welcome back, Lord de Vere. We have quite forgot the fart."[209]

• Lord Melbourne watched a performance of Shakespeare's *Othello*. After Othello had strangled Desdemona, Lord Melbourne remarked, "How different from the private life of our own dear Queen."[210]

Satire

• An unpopular President of the United State can revitalize satire. The last time Erik Henrikson, critic for *The Portland Mercury*, thought that *MAD Magazine* was funny was when he was 12 years old but not after—that is, until George W. Bush, whose incompetence was a boon to all satirists, became President. President Bush especially was a boon to *MAD*, making it cutting edge again as the *MAD* satirists ripped this target apart. For example, *MAD* did a "Where's Waldo?" spoof, asking readers to find "W" after Hurricane Katrina devastated New Orleans. Hint: You can't find him wading through water or camping on rooftops with lots of black people. *MAD* also created a "Handy Glossary to the War on Terror," which defines "collateral damage" as "the official military explanation as to why there are so many empty seats lately in Umm Qasr's fourth-grade classrooms." Mr. Henrikson was mightily impressed and wrote, "I didn't think I'd ever say [that *MAD* was funny again], but the day has come—thanks, *MAD*." By the way, a lot of *MAD*'s Bush-bashing (richly deserved by George W.) has been collected in a book: *The MAD War on Bush*, by the Usual Gang of Idiots.[211]

• *The Smothers Brothers Comedy Hour* was one of the first television shows to engage in political satire—for which it was censored in the form of cancellation despite its popularity. One of the jokes that clean-cut comedians Tom and Dick Smothers made was about the leadership in this country during the Vietnam War. Tom pointed out, "There's a theory of clothes and politics. There's a definite correlation. You can tell who's running the country by how much clothes people wear." This does make sense. People without a lot of money can't afford to buy a lot of clothing, and so they are the less-ons. And, as Tom Smothers pointed out, that means that the people running the country are the more-ons.[212]

• The American experiment is democracy. As Benjamin Franklin observed, we have a republic—as long as we can keep it. (Let me use my First Amendment right of free speech—while I still have it—to say that with the use of easily hackable electronic voting machines, keeping it seems unlikely.) Satirist Mort Sahl once showed up unexpectedly at actor Michael Caine's restaurant in London. Mr. Caine asked, "Mort Sahl? What are you doing in England?" Mr. Sahl replied, "We're back! The experiment failed."[213]

• English music-hall star Marie Lloyd came to America, where she was arrested, detained, and questioned because she arrived in America in the company of a man who was not her husband. Hours later, she was released, and when reporters asked what she thought of America, Ms. Lloyd pointed to the Statue of Liberty and said, "I think your sense of humor is grand."[214]

• The political humor on the 1960s comedy show *Laugh-In* was not always immediately apparent. For example, you have to watch closely to see that when Lily Tomlin's telephone operator character Ernestine dials FBI Director J. Edgar Hoover, she uses her middle finger.[215]

• Political comedian Barry Crimmins had just finished a set in which he had criticized political incompetence when someone told him, "Hey, buddy. America—love it or leave it!" Mr. Crimmins replied, "What? And be a victim of our foreign policy?"[216]

Slavery
• In the days of slavery, a slave mother would sometimes be separated from her children. On a small farm in Tennessee, a slave named Fanny had an infant. Fanny's owner wanted to separate Fanny from her infant. Fanny picked up the infant and threatened to bash its brains out unless her master allowed her to take her baby with her. Her master relented, and Fanny took the infant with her. In another, much less happy story, a slave woman named Margaret Garner tried to escape and run to freedom, taking her children with her. She was recaptured, but she succeeded in killing two of her children first, preferring that they die rather than be returned to slavery.[217]

• As a child, Harriet Tubman was a slave who was beaten often because of her independent nature. She quickly learned to wear extra clothing as padding but to cry and scream as if the blows hurt her. In 1849, she escaped from her owners and gained her freedom in the North, where she became a conductor for the Underground Railroad, guiding escaped slaves from one station to another. This was dangerous work, as she might have been killed if Southerners had caught her helping escaped slaves, but her motto as conductor was, "I can't die but once."[218]

Suffrage

• A horse race at the Epsom Derby in 1913 led to women in England getting the right to vote. Anmer, the favorite to win, was well in the lead in the homestretch when a suffragette named Emily Davidson ran onto the racetrack, shouted "Long live women's suffrage," and threw herself into the path of the horse, which trampled and killed her. Her death gained lots of publicity for women's right to vote, and Parliament quickly passed a law recognizing that right.[219]

• African-American tennis great Arthur Ashe knew how to make a point in an argument. In South Africa, he debated a defender of apartheid. During the argument, he pointed to a grey-headed black man and asked, "Why can't this gentleman vote and you can?" The apartheid defender, a professor from Stellenbosch, replied, "I can't answer that, Mr. Ashe."[220]

Supreme Court

• The United States considers itself a free country, but its freedom has had to be fought for. On July 13, 1958, at 2 a.m. in Central Point, Virginia, Sheriff Garnett Brooks and two deputy sheriffs entered the home of Richard and Mildred Loving, arrested them, and took them to the county jail, where they stayed for five days before being released after posting bail. What crime were they charged with? Mr. Loving was white, and Mrs. Loving was part African American and part Native American. They had fallen in love, gone to Washington, D.C., to get married, then returned to Virginia, which had outlawed marriage between a white person and anyone who was not white. In addition, the state of Virginia had made it illegal for a white person and anyone who was not white to get married in another state, then return to Virginia and live as man and wife. The State of Virginia found Mr. and Mrs. Loving guilty, and Judge Leon M. Bazile sentenced each of them to one year in jail, but he suspended the sentence for 25 years if the Lovings would leave Virginia. In his decision, Judge Bazile made it clear that he opposed marriage between whites and blacks. The Lovings left Virginia for a while, but did not want to be separated from friends and family, so they returned to Virginia. In 1963, Mrs. Loving wrote United States attorney general Robert Kennedy and asked him for help. Mr. Kennedy referred the letter to the American Civil Rights Union, which agreed to represent the Lovings in a lawsuit. Eventually, the case made its way to the United States Supreme Court, and Mr. Loving told his ACLU lawyers, "Tell the court that I love my wife, and it is just unfair that I can't live with her in Virginia." The Supreme Court ruled in favor of the Lovings, making it legal for whites and blacks to marry each other. If the Supreme Court had ruled in favor of the state of Virginia, states would be able to legally ban marriages between white people and non-white people. The Lovings had not set out to be civil rights heroes, but because they loved each other and wanted to legally live together as a married couple in Virginia, they (with the help of the ACLU) refused to let the state of Virginia take away their rights. In doing so, they made possible the Supreme Court ruling that whites and non-whites can legally marry in any state.[221]

• After Ruth Bader Ginsburg became only the second woman to sit on the United States Supreme Court—thanks to Bill Clinton—she was given use of the chambers formerly used by Justice Thurgood Marshall. This was appropriate, as Justice Marshall supported the rights of women. Before becoming a Supreme Court Justice herself, Ms.

Ginsburg had argued six cases before the Supreme Court. She won five of them, and Justice Marshall voted for her clients in all six cases.[222]

Telephones

• The newly elected Pope John XXIII wanted to make a telephone call. In accordance with custom, all communication with the outside world had been cut off, so he had to summon one of the workers of Vatican City to reconnect the telephone. While the worker was making the connection, the two men began to talk. It became apparent that the worker was not aware that he was talking to the newly elected Pope, and soon he began to make honest complaints about the low pay he received at Vatican City—pay that would not adequately support his large family. Soon afterward, a large pay raise of 25 to 40 percent was given to the Vatican City employees. That was done at the expense of direct charitable donations given by the Holy See, but Pope John XXIII felt that it was a simple matter of justice for the Vatican City employees to receive adequate wages. According to Pope John XXIII, "This raise is simple justice, and justice comes before charity."[223]

• When he was a Senator, Lyndon Johnson was one of the first people to get a telephone for his car—something that made Senator Everett Dirksen jealous. Quickly, Senator Dirksen got his own car phone and gave Senator Johnson a call to show that other people had car phones, too. But when Senator Johnson answered the phone, he said, "Just a minute—my other car phone is ringing."[224]

Vice Presidents

• When he was Vice President, Thomas Jefferson once stopped at a fine hotel in Baltimore. However, because he was muddy from riding his horse all day, the hotel management turned him away. Later, the management learned that the muddy "farmer" they had turned away was the Vice President of the United States, and so they searched for him to tell him they would be honored if he would stay at their hotel. However, after they located Mr. Jefferson, he told them, "If you have no room for a muddy farmer, you shall have none for this Vice President."[225]

• When he was Vice President, Walter F. Mondale used to tell a story about a woman being interviewed on the radio. She lived near Three Mile Island, and after being evacuated because of the disaster, she couldn't wait to go back home. The interviewer asked her if she wasn't afraid to go back. She replied, "No, not at all. The President was here the other day—if there was any danger, they would have sent the Vice President." At this point, Vice President Mondale would tell the audience, "Well, here I am."[226]

Voting

• Susan B. Anthony believed, "It was we, the people, not we, the white male citizens, nor we, the male citizens; but we, the whole people, who formed this Union." Because of her belief, she knew that women have the right to vote, despite being forbidden to exercise their right by the unjust laws of her day. In Rochester, New York, on election day of the 1872 Presidential race, she led a group of women to the polls to vote, but was arrested and thrown into prison. Despite being fined for her act of civil disobedience, Ms. Anthony refused to pay the fine. Wisely, the authorities never attempted to collect it.[227]

• Ralph Nader's father, Nathra, disliked political posturing by both the Republicans and the Democrats. One thing that he said often was this: "When asked whether I am a Republican or a Democrat, I reply that I am an American." He once sued the Democratic Party in Connecticut because he felt that independents ought to be able to vote in the Democratic Party primary because the primary election was being held with taxpayer money. He lost the case.[228]

War

• During World War I, Alvin York was a conscientious objector, based on his strongly held religious beliefs. Drafted into the United States Army, he tried four times to be classified as a conscientious objector, but he failed each time. Finally, he talked to Major George

Buxton, a devout Christian who recognized Mr. York's sincerity. He asked Mr. York if he believed the Bible, and Mr. York replied, "Every sentence, every word." Major Buxton then quoted Luke 22.36: "He that hath no sword, let him sell his cloak and buy one." He also reminded Mr. York about what Jesus had done when he found moneylenders in the temple. Finally, he asked what Jesus would do when the enemy threatened friends and families. Mr. York asked for a pass to think things through, and he went home to rural Tennessee on March 21, 1918. Near Pall Mall, Tennessee, he climbed a mountain and stayed there to pray for two days and two nights. Then he went to war overseas. On October 8, 1918, Corporal York and a small group of American soldiers were fired on by German machine gunners. Corporal York used his hunting skills to shoot several German machine gunners. When he and his men were attacked by a German officer and a dozen soldiers who charged them with bayonets, he killed all of them with an automatic pistol, the furthest away one first and the nearest one last. This was the same order in which he shot wild turkeys at home, since he didn't want the ones in front to know that the others had been killed. Then he began shooting machine gunners again. After Corporal York had shot approximately twenty of the machine gunners, the remaining Germans gave up and surrendered—except for one soldier who threw a grenade at Corporal York. The soldier missed, and Corporal York shot him. On the way back to the Allied lines, Corporal York and his men captured more and more Germans, ending up with a total of 132 soldiers, including four officers. Once everyone was safely in camp, an Allied officer told him, "Well, York, I hear you have captured the whole d*mned German army." For his efforts, Corporal York was promoted to Sergeant and awarded the Medal of Honor.[229]

• When the United States was fighting the war in Vietnam, a sergeant wrote famed photographer Yousuf Karsh and requested a copy of a portrait that he had taken of Eleanor Roosevelt. Mr. Karsh wondered why a young man would be interested in a portrait of a woman who had been First Lady before he was born, so he wrote the soldier. As it turned out, the soldier was not young, but instead he was a career soldier who had been wounded in the Korean War. Ms. Roosevelt had visited him and many other wounded soldiers. Of course, Ms. Roosevelt was not a great beauty, but she was a great human being who genuinely cared for other people. She showed genuine concern for this soldier and other soldiers. The soldier wrote Mr. Karsh, "When she came in, I thought she was the homeliest woman I ever seen—and when she left, the most beautiful."[230]

• Technical sergeant Leonard Matlovich had impressive military credentials. He won the Bronze Star, two Purple Hearts, an air force Meritorious Service Medal, and two air force commendations. In addition, he served two tours of duty in Vietnam during his 11 years of outstanding service in the military. However, he was gay, and because he was gay, he was dismissed from the military. Later, after a long legal battle, the Pentagon gave him $160,000 to stay out of the military. On the advice of his lawyers, he took the money. When he died of AIDS, his tombstone (which he had designed) stated, "A Gay Vietnam Veteran" and "When I was in the military, they gave me a medal for killing two men and a discharge for loving one."[231]

• Children react to funerals in different ways. Herbert Eisenmann, a German soldier, and Hank Werkman, an American soldier, each had a leg amputated above the knee as a result of shrapnel wounds suffered during World War II. Both endured phantom pain, for which a physician would inject a painkiller into their stump. Mr. Eisenmann was buried without his prosthesis, which his government asked to be returned to it as the prosthesis was government property. Mr. Werkman was buried with his prosthesis. Inge, Mr. Eisenmann's daughter, worried that her father might need his prosthesis. Beth, Mr. Werkman's daughter, hoped that her father would not need his prosthesis.[232]

• During World War II, the Germans conquered France and forced the French to work for them, including forcing them to make bombs to use against the British. The French resisted by deliberately making duds that would not explode. One bomb fell on the Cathedral at Canterbury. The wife of the Most Reverend William Temple, Archbishop of Canterbury, said, "It did not explode, and when we finally examined it, we saw written on it a message, '*Vive la France.*' We knew then that it was one of the duds that French patriots, enslaved by the Nazis, are making at the risk of their lives."[233]

• Dr. Thomas R.P. Dawson survived the Japanese occupation of Malaysia during World War II. Just before the takeover, he decided to visit his barber. The air raid siren blew during his haircut, and he and his barber went to an air raid shelter. Later, they returned to the barbershop, when once again the siren blew. Again, they went to an air raid shelter, and again, they returned to the barbershop, and again, the siren blew. Before Dr. Dawson received a complete hair cut, he and his barber had visited the air raid shelter four times.[234]

• Youthful attitudes toward war can be very naïve. For example, during World War II, German young people were excited when bombs fell on Cologne for the first time, even though people were hurt. Geerte Murmann writes about kids looking for pieces of shrapnel and regarding them as prized possessions. She was in Bavaria, away from Cologne, when the first Allied bombs fell, and she was disappointed that she wasn't in Cologne. She wrote a friend, "Finally something terrific is happening in Cologne, and I'm not there."[235]

• During the McCarthy era, a lot of actors went overboard in worrying about Communists, but fortunately a few actors kept their perspective. One actor who kept his perspective was Russell Johnson, who played the Professor on *Gilligan's Island*. While guest starring on *The Real McCoys*, he was asked by Walter Brennan, who feared Communists, to sign a loyalty oath. Mr. Russell—who had been awarded a Purple Heart while flying in World War II—declined.[236]

• The first official Christian nation in the world is Armenia. When King Tiridates III (died 330 C.E.) became a convert to Christianity, Armenia's citizens soon converted, also. They were serious about their religion. When the Persians conquered part of Armenia and ordered the Armenians to convert to Zoroastrianism, which the Persians followed, the Armenians rebelled. After 20 years of war, the Persians relented and permitted the Armenians to remain Christian.[237]

• According to historian Arthur M. Schlesinger, Jr., Barbara Tuchman's book *The Guns of August* once prevented what might have been another world war. President John F. Kennedy read the book during the Cuban missile crisis, and after reading how World War I had started as a result of the advice of the hard-line, bone-headed military experts of that time, he resisted taking advice from the hard-line, bone-headed military experts of his own time.[238]

• Modern Americans don't realize how horrible war is because it has been so long since a war was fought on American soil. During World War II, gunfire killed a horse on a street in Buda, Hungary. Quickly, starving civilians stripped the flesh from the horse so they would have something to eat. Swedish diplomat Per Anger and other Swedes were grateful that the horse goulash they cooked lasted for a few days.[239]

• Behind the scenes of the hit sitcom *Roseanne*, a power struggle raged as star Roseanne wrestled control of the show away from executive producer Matt Williams. In the turmoil, many writers either quit or were fired, and one former writer for Roseanne paid for an advertisement in *Variety* that announced that he was planning a vacation "in the relative peace and quiet of Beirut."[240]

• After the battle of Gettysburg on July 1-3, 1863, a Union soldier lay wounded on the battlefield as the defeated Confederate general Robert E. Lee rode by in retreat. The Union soldier shouted out, "Hurrah for the Union!" General Lee dismounted, walked over the soldier, grabbed his hand, and said, "My son, I hope that you will soon be well."[241]

• As a child, Bulgarian-born Sonia Arova studied ballet in Paris. In 1940, with the Nazis ready to take control of Paris, she needed to escape, so her parents enlisted the help of an English couple whose son was not traveling with them. Young Sonia cut her hair short, pretended to be the English couple's son, and escaped from Paris.[242]

• Many of us are fortunate because we don't know what war is like. During World War II, Rudolf Bing worked in London. Following a bombing attack, he saw a girl's arm in a pile of rubble and he pulled at it. The arm came out of the rubble—the other pieces of the girl were elsewhere.[243]

Women's Rights

• In the 1820s, in Johnstown, New York, a woman named Flora Campbell lived on a farm that had once belonged to her parents. Living with her were her husband and her son. When the husband died, he left the farm in his will to their son. The son then ordered Mrs. Campbell, his mother, off the property. Wondering what rights she had in this matter, Mrs. Campbell consulted the lawyer Daniel Cady, who informed her that legally a woman's husband owned whatever property she had and that legally he could will it to whichever person he wished. Mr. Cady's daughter, Elizabeth, overheard this conversation. She thought that the law was "mean" and therefore she wanted to use scissors to cut it out of her father's law book. However, her father explained that this action would do little good. The law needed to be changed, and making that change would take an action by the legislature. As an adult, Elizabeth—better known as Elizabeth Cady Stanton—became a forceful and effective advocate of women's rights.[244]

• Emmeline Pankhurst was a crusader for women's suffrage in England, but she learned a lot from a fellow activist: Christabel, her daughter. For a long time, Emmeline tried to politely advocate women's rights, but she was ignored. But in 1905, Christabel, accompanied by a friend, attended a speech by a politician. During the question-and-answer session, Christabel and her friend asked, "Will the government give votes to women?" The politician ignored the question, so Christabel and her friend asked it again and again. Eventually, Christabel and her friend were arrested, and suddenly newspapers began writing about women's suffrage. Emmeline realized that in order to get the topic of women's rights noticed by the newspapers, she had to quit being polite. Thereafter, Emmeline, Christabel, and Sylvia (another daughter) were arrested many, many times (as were Mahatma Gandhi and Martin Luther King, Jr., later). By the time Emmeline died, women had the vote in England.[245]

• Lady Astor, the first female Member of Parliament, had an acid tongue. Winston Churchill did not think that women should be Members of Parliament, and he told her that a woman's walking into Parliament disturbed him exactly the same way it would if a woman were to walk into a bathroom he was occupying. She replied, "You are not handsome enough to have such fears." And when he asked her for advice about which disguise to wear to a costumed ball, she replied, "Why don't you come sober, Mr. Prime Minister?"[246]

Work

• During World War II, Lady Reading became chair of the Women's Voluntary Services for Air Raid Precautions in England. She helped recruit over a million volunteers, who performed such services as organizing communal feeding centers, baking and delivering pies (a forerunner of Meals on Wheels), and knitting woolen clothing for people living in the liberated areas of Europe. Although she was the head of the organization, no insignia told her rank; therefore, when she stopped at a canteen, she was ordered to help out by washing dishes. (She obeyed the order.)[247]

• In 1898, Thomas B. Reed campaigned to be the Republican candidate in the Presidential election. One day, the wife and the young son of Ellison Purdy, who was the pastor of the Oak Street Meeting in Portland, Maine, walked past Mr. Reed's house. The young son, Alex, asked his mother, "Tom Reed wants to be President, doesn't he?" Mrs. Purdy replied affirmatively. Young Alex then asked, "Will my father ever be President?" Mrs. Purdy replied, "No, thy father is a preacher—he has a job."[248]

• At the request of physicist Albert Einstein, the International Rescue Committee was founded in 1933 to help refugees. IRC caseworker Lang Ngan helps refugees arriving in New York City. In her job, she helps families learn all about life in the United States and has taught them such things as how to ride the subway, how to open savings and checking accounts at a bank, and even how to flush a toilet.[249]

• Being a Supreme Court Justice can be a time-consuming job. Justice Ruth Bader Ginsburg sometimes reads legal briefs while sitting in a restaurant and waiting for friends to arrive. In addition, she sometimes reads papers with a flashlight in a movie theater while the Coming Attractions are displayed on the movie screen.[250]

Appendix A: Bibliography

Addiss, Stephen, and G. Cameron Hurst III. *Samurai Painters*. Tokyo: Kodansha International, Ltd., 1983.

Adler, Bill. *Jewish Wit and Wisdom*. New York: Dell Publishing Co., Inc, 1969.

Alonso, Karen. Loving v. Virginia*: Interracial Marriage*. Berkeley Heights, NJ: Enslow Publications, Inc., 2000.

Alpern, Hyman. *Teachers are Funny*. South Brunswick and New York: A.S. Barnes and Co., 1968.

Altman, Linda Jacobs. *Genocide: The Systematic Killing of a People*. Springfield, NJ: Enslow Publications, Inc., 1995.

Altman, Linda Jacobs. *Slavery and Abolition in American History*. Berkeley Heights, NJ: Enslow Publications, Inc., 1999.

Anflick, Charles. *Resistance: Teen Partisans and Resisters Who Fought Nazi Tyranny*. New York: The Rosen Publishing Group, Inc., 1999.

Ayer, Eleanor H. *In the Ghettos: Teens Who Survived the Ghettos of the Holocaust*. New York: The Rosen Publishing Group, Inc., 1999.

Barter, James. *Julius Caesar and Ancient Rome in World History*. Berkeley Heights, NJ: Enslow Publications, Inc., 2001.

Bernard, Catherine. *Sojourner Truth: Abolitionist and Women's Rights Activist*. Berkeley Heights, NJ: Enslow Publications, Inc., 2001.

Biggers, Don Hampton. *Buffalo Guns & Barbed Wire*. Lubbock, TX: Texas Tech University Press, 1991.

Bing, Sir Rudolf. *5000 Nights at the Opera*. Garden City, NY: Doubleday and Company, Inc., 1972.

Bing, Sir Rudolf. *A Knight at the Opera*. New York: G.P. Putnam's Sons, 1981.

Bredeson, Carmen. *Ruth Bader Ginsburg: Supreme Court Justice*. Springfield, NJ: Enslow Publications, Inc., 1995.

Brown, Michèle and Ann O'Connor. *Hammer and Tongues: A Dictionary of Women's Wit and Humour*. London: J.M. Dent and Sons, Ltd., 1986.

Brunsting, Bernard R. *Laugh!!! Your Health May Depend on It*. Columbus, GA: Quill Publications, 1995.

Bryce, Ivar. *You Only Live Once: Memories of Ian Fleming*. London: Weidenfeld and Nicolson, 1984.

Burger, Leslie, and Debra L. Rahm. *United Nations High Commissioner for Refugees: Making a Difference in Our World*. Minneapolis, MN: Lerner Publications Company, 1996.

Charles, Helen White, collector and editor. *Quaker Chuckles and Other True Stories About Friends*. Oxford, OH: H.W. Charles, 1961.

Cheatham, Kae. *Dennis Banks: Native American Activist*. Springfield, NJ: Enslow Publications, Inc., 1997.

Chenevière, Alain. *Ramachandra in India*. Minneapolis, MN: Lerner Publications Company, 1996.

Chernow, Ron. *The Death of the Banker*. New York: Vintage Books, 1997.

Clercq, Tanaquil Le. *The Ballet Cook Book*. New York: Stein and Day, Publishers, 1966.

Clinton, Kate. *What the L?* New York: Carroll & Graf Publishers, 2005.

Cole, Michael D. *The* Titanic: *Disaster at Sea*. Berkeley Heights, NJ. Enslow Publications, Inc., 2001.

Cooke, Alistair. *The Great and the Good*. New York: Arcade Publishing, 1999.

Currie, Stephen. *We Have Marched Together: The Working Children's Crusade*. Minneapolis, MN: Lerner Publications Company, 1997.

Cytron, Barry and Phyllis. *Myriam Mendilow: Mother of Jerusalem*. Minneapolis, MN: Lerner Publications Company, 1994.

Darby, Jean. *Martin Luther King, Jr.* Minneapolis, MN: Lerner Publications Company, 1990.

Davis, Mac. *Strange and Incredible Sports Happenings*. New York: Grosset and Dunlap, Publishers, 1975.

Davis, Mary L. *Women Who Changed History: Five Famous Queens of Europe*. Minneapolis, MN: Lerner Publications Company, 1974.

Dawson, Thomas R.P. *Amusing Sidelights on Japanese Occupation*. 2nd ed. Petaling Jaya, Selangor, Malaysia: Thomas Dawson, 1972.

Dick, Philip K. *I Hope I Shall Arrive Soon*. Edited by Mark Hurst and Paul Williams. Garden City, NY: Doubleday, 1985.

Doherty, Kieran. *Congressional Medal of Honor Recipients*. Springfield, NJ: Enslow Publications, Inc., 1998.

Dole, Bob. *Great Political Wit*. New York: Doubleday, 1998.

Dole, Bob. *Great Presidential Wit*. New York: Scribner, 2001.

Dvorson, Alexa. *The Hitler Youth: Marching Toward Madness*. New York: The Rosen Publishing Group, Inc., 1999.

Ebert, Roger; Daniel Curley, and Jack Lane. *The Perfect London Walk*. Kansas City, MO: Andrews and McMeel, 1986.

Edwards, Judith. *Lewis and Clark's Journey of Discovery in American History*. Springfield, NJ: Enslow Publications, Inc., 1999.

Epstein, Lawrence J. *Mixed Nuts: America's Love Affair with Comedy Teams From Burns and Allen to Belushi and Aykroyd*. New York: PublicAffairs, 2004.

Feinberg, David B. *Queer and Loathing: Rants and Raves of a Raging AIDS Clone*. New York: Viking, 1994.

Ferguson, John, compiler and translator. *The Wit of the Greeks and Romans*. London: Leslie Frewin, 1968.

Fletcher, Lynne Yamaguchi. *The First Gay Pope and Other Records*. Boston, MA: Alyson Publications, Inc., 1992.

Floyd, E. Randall. *The Good, the Bad, and the Mad: Weird People in American History*. Augusta, GA: Harbor House, 1999.

Flynn, Tom, and Karen Lound. *AIDS: Examining the Crisis*. Minneapolis, MN: Lerner Publications Company, 1995.

Ford, Michael Thomas. *The Voices of AIDS: Twelve Unforgettable People Talk About How AIDS has Changed Their Lives*. New York: Morrow Junior Books, 1995.

Fountain, Richard, compiler. *The Wit of the Wig*. London: Leslie Frewin Publishers, Limited, 1968.

Fremon, David K. *The Great Depression in American History*. Springfield, NJ: Enslow Publications, Inc., 1997.

Fremon, David K. *The Holocaust Heroes*. Springfield, NJ: Enslow Publications, Inc., 1998.

Fuller, Gerald. *Stories for All Seasons*. Mystic, CT: Twenty-Third Publications, 1996.

Galas, Judith C. *Gay Rights*. San Diego, CA: Lucent Books, 1996.

Garner, Joe. *Made You Laugh: the Funniest Moments in Radio, Television, Stand-up, and Movie Comedy*. Kansas City, MO: Andrews McMeel Publishing, 2004.

Garvey, Rev. Francis J. *Favorite Humor of Famous Americans*. Kandiyohi, MN: Rev. Francis J. Garvey, 1981.

Gaster, Moses. *The Exempla of the Rabbis: Being a Collection of Exempla, Apologues and Tales Culled from Hebrew Manuscripts and Rare Hebrew Books*. New York: Ktav Publishing House, Inc., 1968.

Gerler, William R. *Educator's Treasurer of Humor for All Occasions*. West Nyack, NY: Parker Publishing Company, 1972.

Gershick, Zsa Zsa. *Gay Old Girls*. Los Angeles, CA: Alyson Books, 1998.

Gingras, Angele de T. *From Bussing to Bugging: The Best in Congressional Humor*. Washington, D.C.: Acropolis Books, Limited, 1973.

Gonzales, Doreen. *AIDS: Ten Stories of Courage*. Springfield, NJ: Enslow Publications, Inc., 1996.

Gray, Bettyanne. *Manya's Story*. Minneapolis, MN: Lerner Publications Company, 1978.

Green, Carl R., and William R. Sanford. *Judge Roy Bean*. Springfield, NJ: Enslow Publications, Inc., 1995.

Greenspan, Bud. *100 Greatest Moments in Olympic History*. Los Angeles, CA: General Publishing Group, Inc., 1995.

Guernsey, JoAnn Bren. *Voices of Feminism: Past, Present, and Future*. Minneapolis, MN: Lerner Publications Company, 1996.

Hacker, Carlotta. *Humanitarians*. New York: Crabtree Publishing Company, 1999.

Hacker, Carlotta. *Rebels*. New York: Crabtree Publishing Company, 1999.

Hadleigh, Boze. *Hollywood Gays*. New York: Barricade Books, Inc., 1996.

Halamandaris, Val, editor and compiler. *Faces of Caring*. Washington, D.C.: Caring Publishing, 1992.

Harmon, Ron L. *American Civil Rights Leaders*. Berkeley Heights, NJ: Enslow Publications, Inc., 2000.

Haskins, Jim, and N.R. Mitgang. *Mr. Bojangles: The Story of Bill Robinson*. New York: William Morrow and Company, Inc., 1988.

Henry, Lewis C. *Humorous Anecdotes About Famous People*. Garden City, NY: Halcyon House, 1948.

Henry, Sondra, and Emily Taitz. *Betty Friedan: Fighter for Women's Rights*. Hillside, NJ: Enslow Publications, Inc., 1990.

Herda, D.J. *Thurgood Marshall: Civil Rights Champion*. Springfield, NJ: Enslow Publications, Inc., 1995.

Hicks, Bill. *Love All the People: Letters, Lyrics, Routines*. Brooklyn, NY: Soft Skull Press, 2004.

Hintz, Martin. *Farewell, John Barleycorn: Prohibition in the United States*. Minneapolis, MN: Lerner Publications Company, 1996.

Hoff, Benjamin. *The Tao of Pooh*. New York: Penguin Books, 1982.

Hollingsworth, Amy. *The Simple Faith of Mister Rogers*. Nashville, TN: Integrity Publishers, 2005.

Jacobson, Steve. *Carrying Jackie's Torch: The Players Who Integrated Baseball—and America*. Chicago, IL: Lawrence Hill Books, 2007.

Johnson, Russell, and Steve Cox. *Here on Gilligan's Isle*. New York: HarperCollins Publishers, Inc., 1993.

Josephson, Judith Pinkerton. *Allan Pinkerton: The Original Private Eye*. Minneapolis, MN: Lerner Publications Company, 1996.

Josephson, Judith Pinkerton. *Mother Jones: Fierce Fighter for Workers' Rights*. Minneapolis, MN: Lerner Publications Company, 1997.

Kafka, Tina. *Gay Rights*. Farmington Hills, MI: Lucent Books, 2006.

Kanner, Bernice. *The 100 Best TV Commercials ... and Why They Worked*. New York: Times Books, 1999.

Karsh, Yousuf. *Faces of Destiny: Portraits by Karsh*. Chicago, IL: Ziff-Davis Publishing Company, 1946.

Karsh, Yousuf. *Karsh: A Sixty-Year Retrospective*. Boston, MA: Little, Brown and Company, 1996.

Keller, Emily. *Margaret Bourke-White: A Photographer's Life*. Minneapolis, MN: Lerner Publications Company, 1996.

Kendall, Martha E. *Failure is Impossible! The History of American Women's Rights*. Minneapolis, MN: Lerner Publications Company, 2001.

Kertzer, Morris N. *Tell Me, Rabbi*. New York: Bloch Publishing Company, 1976.

Kolasky, John, collector and compiler. *Look, Comrade—The People are Laughing ....* Toronto, Ontario: Peter Martin Associates, Limited, 1972.

Lee, Stan, and George Mair. *Excelsior! The Amazing Life of Stan Lee*. New York: Fireside, 2002.

Lipsyte, Robert. *Assignment: Sports*. New York: Harper & Row, Publishers, 1984.

McArthur, Debra. *Raoul Wallenberg: Rescuing Thousands from the Nazis' Grasp*. Berkeley Heights, NJ: Enslow Publishers, Inc., 2005.

Medearis, Angela Shelf, and Michael R. Medearis. *Dance*. New York: Twenty-First Century Books, 1997.

Michaels, Louis. *The Humor and Warmth of Pope John XXIII: His Anecdotes and Legends*. New York: Pocket Books, Inc., 1965.

Miller, John, editor. *Legends: Women Who Have Changed the World*. Novato, CA: New World Books, 1998.

Miller, John and Kirsten. *Legends 2: Women Who Have Changed the World, Through the Eyes of Great Women Writers*. Novato, CA: New World Library, 2004.

Moore, Michael. *Downsize This!* New York: HarperPerennial, 1997.

Nachman, Gerald. *Seriously Funny: The Rebel Comedians of the 1950s and 1960s*. New York: Pantheon Books, 2003.

Nader, Rose B. and Nathra. *It Happened in the Kitchen: Recipes for Food and Thought*. Washington, D.C.: Center for Study of Responsive Law, 1991.

Ohio University Emeriti Association, compilers. *Ohio University Recollections for the Bicentennial Anniversary: 1804-2004*. Athens, OH: Ohio University, 2004.

Orleans, Ellen. *Can't Keep a Straight Face*. Bala Cynwyd, PA: Laugh Lines Press, 1992.

Orleans, Ellen. *Still Can't Keep a Straight Face*. Bala Cynwyd, PA: Laugh Lines Press, 1996.

Osborne, Angela. *Abigail Adams: Women's Rights Advocate*. New York: Chelsea House Publishers, 1989.

Ravitch, Diane, ed. *The American Reader: Words That Moved a Nation*. New York: HarperCollins Publishers, 1990.

Reynolds, Moira Davison. *Women Champions of Human Rights*. Jefferson, NC: McFarland and Company, Inc., 1991.

Rolph, Daniel N. *My Brother's Keeper: Union and Confederate Soldiers' Acts of Mercy during the Civil War*. Mechanicsburg, PA: Stackpole Books, 2002.

Ruksenas, Algis. *Is That You Laughing Comrade? The World's Best Russian (Underground) Jokes*. Secaucus, NJ: Citadel Press, 1986.

Rutkowska, Wanda. *Famous People in Anecdotes*. Warszawa: Wydawnictwa Szkolne i Pedagogiczne, 1977.

Salzberg, Sharon. *Lovingkindness: The Revolutionary Art of Happiness*. Boston, MA: Shambhala Publications, Inc., 1995.

Samra, Cal and Rose, editors. *More Holy Humor*. Colorado Springs, CO: WaterBrook Press, 1997.

Sapieha, Virgilia, Ruth Neely, and Mary Love Collins. *Eminent Women: Recipients of the National Achievement Award*. Menasha, WI: George Banta Publishing Company, 1948.

Shindler, Phyllis, collector. *Raise Your Glasses*. London: Judy Piatkus, Limited, 1988.

Shore, Nancy. *Amelia Earhart*. New York: Chelsea House Publishers, 1987.

Smith, H. Allen. *Buskin' With H. Allen Smith*. New York: Trident Press, 1968.

Smith, H. Allen. *Lo, the Former Egyptian!* Garden City, NY: Doubleday & Co., Inc., 1947.

Sobol, Donald J. *Encyclopedia Brown's Book of Wacky Cars*. New York: William Morrow and Company, Inc., 1987.

Sobol, Donald J. *Encyclopedia Brown's Book of Wacky Sports*. New York: William Morrow and Company, 1984.

Spencer, John. *Workers for Humanity*. London: George G. Harrap and Co., Ltd., 1962.

Terry, Walter. *Frontiers of Dance: The Life of Martha Graham*. New York: Thomas Y. Crowell Company, 1975.

Towle, Mike. *I Remember Arthur Ashe*. Nashville, TN: Cumberland House, 2001.

Tracy, Kathleen. *The Life and Times of Confucius*. Hockessin, DE: Mitchell Lane Publishers, Inc., 2005.

Trillin, Calvin. *About Alice*. New York: Random House, 2006.

Van Dyke, Dick. *Those Funny Kids!* Garden City, NY: Doubleday and Company, Inc., 1975.

Wordsworth, R.D., compiler. *"Abe" Lincoln's Anecdotes and Stories*. Boston, MA: The Mutual Book Company, 1908.

Wulffson, Don L. *Amazing True Stories*. New York: Cobblehill Books, 1991.

Appendix B: About the Author

It was a dark and stormy night. Suddenly a cry rang out, and on a hot summer night in 1954, Josephine, wife of Carl Bruce, gave birth to a boy—me. Unfortunately, this young married couple allowed Reuben Saturday, Josephine's brother, to name their first-born. Reuben, aka "The Joker," decided that Bruce was a nice name, so he decided to name me Bruce Bruce. I have gone by my middle name—David—ever since.

Being named Bruce David Bruce hasn't been all bad. Bank tellers remember me very quickly, so I don't often have to show an ID. It can be fun in charades, also. When I was a counselor as a teenager at Camp Echoing Hills in Warsaw, Ohio, a fellow counselor gave the signs for "sounds like" and "two words," then she pointed to a bruise on her leg twice. Bruise Bruise? Oh yeah, Bruce Bruce is the answer!

Uncle Reuben, by the way, gave me a haircut when I was in kindergarten. He cut my hair short and shaved a small bald spot on the back of my head. My mother wouldn't let me go to school until the bald spot grew out again.

Of all my brothers and sisters (six in all), I am the only transplant to Athens, Ohio. I was born in Newark, Ohio, and have lived all around Southeastern Ohio. However, I moved to Athens to go to Ohio University and have never left.

At Ohio U, I never could make up my mind whether to major in English or Philosophy, so I got a bachelor's degree with a double major in both areas, then I added a Master of Arts degree in English and a Master of Arts degree in Philosophy. Yes, I have my MAMA degree.

Currently, and for a long time to come (I eat fruits and veggies), I am spending my retirement writing books such as *Nadia Comaneci: Perfect 10*, *The Funniest People in Comedy*, *Homer's* Iliad: *A Retelling in Prose*, and *William Shakespeare's* Hamlet: *A Retelling in Prose*.

If all goes well, I will publish one or two books a year for the rest of my life. (On the other hand, a good way to make God laugh is to tell Her your plans.)

By the way, my sister Brenda Kennedy writes romances such as *A New Beginning* and *Shattered Dreams*.

Appendix C: Some Books by David Bruce

Anecdote Collections

250 Anecdotes About Opera
250 Anecdotes About Religion
250 Anecdotes About Religion: Volume 2
250 Music Anecdotes
Be a Work of Art: 250 Anecdotes and Stories
The Coolest People in Art: 250 Anecdotes
The Coolest People in the Arts: 250 Anecdotes
The Coolest People in Books: 250 Anecdotes
The Coolest People in Comedy: 250 Anecdotes
Create, Then Take a Break: 250 Anecdotes
Don't Fear the Reaper: 250 Anecdotes
The Funniest People in Art: 250 Anecdotes
The Funniest People in Books: 250 Anecdotes
The Funniest People in Books, Volume 2: 250 Anecdotes
The Funniest People in Books, Volume 3: 250 Anecdotes
The Funniest People in Comedy: 250 Anecdotes
The Funniest People in Dance: 250 Anecdotes
The Funniest People in Families: 250 Anecdotes
The Funniest People in Families, Volume 2: 250 Anecdotes
The Funniest People in Families, Volume 3: 250 Anecdotes
The Funniest People in Families, Volume 4: 250 Anecdotes
The Funniest People in Families, Volume 5: 250 Anecdotes
The Funniest People in Families, Volume 6: 250 Anecdotes
The Funniest People in Movies: 250 Anecdotes
The Funniest People in Music: 250 Anecdotes
The Funniest People in Music, Volume 2: 250 Anecdotes
The Funniest People in Music, Volume 3: 250 Anecdotes
The Funniest People in Neighborhoods: 250 Anecdotes
The Funniest People in Relationships: 250 Anecdotes
The Funniest People in Sports: 250 Anecdotes
The Funniest People in Sports, Volume 2: 250 Anecdotes
The Funniest People in Television and Radio: 250 Anecdotes
The Funniest People in Theater: 250 Anecdotes

The Funniest People Who Live Life: 250 Anecdotes
The Funniest People Who Live Life, Volume 2: 250 Anecdotes
The Kindest People Who Do Good Deeds, Volume 1: 250 Anecdotes
The Kindest People Who Do Good Deeds, Volume 2: 250 Anecdotes
Maximum Cool: 250 Anecdotes
The Most Interesting People in Movies: 250 Anecdotes
The Most Interesting People in Politics and History: 250 Anecdotes
The Most Interesting People in Politics and History, Volume 2: 250 Anecdotes
The Most Interesting People in Politics and History, Volume 3: 250 Anecdotes
The Most Interesting People in Religion: 250 Anecdotes
The Most Interesting People in Sports: 250 Anecdotes
The Most Interesting People Who Live Life: 250 Anecdotes
The Most Interesting People Who Live Life, Volume 2: 250 Anecdotes
Reality is Fabulous: 250 Anecdotes and Stories
Resist Psychic Death: 250 Anecdotes
Seize the Day: 250 Anecdotes and Stories

[1]Source: Ron L. Harmon, *American Civil Rights Leaders*, pp. 24-25, 81-82.

[2] Source: Kate Clinton, *What the L?*, pp. 27-29.

[3]Source: Amy Hollingsworth, *The Simple Faith of Mister Rogers*, pp. 94-95.

[4] Source: Greg Bluestein, "Creators put politics into video games." 21 January 2007 <http://news.yahoo.com/s/ap/20070122/ap_on_hi_te/opinion_games>.

[5]Source: Sondra Henry and Emily Taitz, *Betty Friedan: Fighter for Women's Rights*, pp. 63, 75-77.

[6] Source: Tina Kafka, *Gay Rights*, pp. 11-12, 15.

[7] Source: Bud Greenspan, *100 Greatest Moments in Olympic History*, pp. 84-85.

[8]Source: Ron L. Harmon, *American Civil Rights Leaders*, pp. 42-45.

[9]Source: Sondra Henry and Emily Taitz, *Betty Friedan: Fighter for Women's Rights*, pp. 68-70.

[10]Source: Stephen Currie, *We Have Marched Together: The Working Children's Crusade*, pp. 26-27.

[11] Source: Thomas R.P. Dawson, *Amusing Sidelights on Japanese Occupation*, p. 29.

[12] Source: Algis Ruksenas, *Is That You Laughing Comrade?*, p. 101.

[13] Source: David B. Feinberg, *Queer and Loathing: Rants and Raves of a Raging AIDS Clone*, pp. 254-257.

[14] Source: Jim Haskins and N.R. Mitgang, *Mr. Bojangles*, p. 222.

[15] Source: Barry and Phyllis Cytron, *Myriam Mendilow: Mother of Jerusalem*, pp. 95ff.

[16]Source: Kae Cheatham, *Dennis Banks: Native American Activist*, p. 28.

[17] Source: "Germaine Greer, "Happy birthday, Sydney Harbour bridge. It's time your designer got the credit he deserves." *The Guardian*. 26 March 2007 <http://www.guardian.co.uk/g2/story/0,,2042743,00.html>.

[18]Source: Ellen Orleans, *Can't Keep a Straight Face*, pp. 20-21.

[19] Source: *The Economist*, "From Hermes to bonsai kittens." Dec. 20, 2005 <http://economist.com/world/
displaystory.cfm?story_id=5323412&no_na_tran=1>.

[20] Source: JoAnn Bren Guernsey, *Voices of Feminism: Past, Present, and Future*, p. 10.

[21]Source: Bernice Kanner, *The 100 Best TV Commercials*, pp. 114-115.

[22]Source: Morris N. Kertzer, *Tell Me, Rabbi*, p. 84.

[23]Source: Sharon Salzberg, *Lovingkindness*, p. 48.

[24] Source: Molly Ivins, "Remembering Ann Richards." 15 September 2006 <http://www.alternet.org/story/41688/>.

[25] Source: David B. Feinberg, *Queer and Loathing: Rants and Raves of a Raging AIDS Clone*, pp. 260-265.

[26] Source: Tom Flynn and Karen Lound, *AIDS: Examining the Crisis*, p. 49.

[27] Source: Michael Thomas Ford, *The Voices of AIDS*, pp. 97-98.

[28]Source: H. Allen Smith, *Lo, the Former Egyptian!*, p. 186.

[29] Source: Phyllis Shindler, collector, *Raise Your Glasses*, p. 101.

[30] Source: Roger Ebert and Daniel Curley, *The Perfect London Walk*, p. 79.

[31]Source: Martin Hintz, *Farewell, John Barleycorn: Prohibition in the United States*, pp. 81, 83.

[32] Source: Yousuf Karsh, *Karsh: A Sixty-Year Retrospective*, p. 54.

[33] Source: H. Allen Smith, *Buskin' With H. Allen Smith*, p. 83.

[34] Source: Kevin Maher, "Taking it on the chin." *The Times*. 14 April 2007 <http://entertainment.timesonline.co.uk/tol/arts_and_entertainment/film/article1639682.ece>.

[35] Source: Gerald Nachman, *Seriously Funny*, pp. 137-138.

[36]Source: Leslie Burger and Debra L. Rahm, *United Nations High Commissioner for Refugees: Making a Difference in Our World*, pp. 50, 69.

[37] Source: "From lesbian vets to Donatella Versace." *The Guardian*. 17 November 2006 <http://www.guardian.co.uk/g2/story/0,,1950165,00.html>.

[38] Source: Emily Keller, *Margaret Bourke-White: A Photographer's Life*, pp. 101-102.

[39] Source: Beth Quinn, "In memory of one fine Texan's wit and wisdom." 25 September 2006 <http://www.recordonline.com/apps/pbcs.dll/article?AID=/20060925/NEWS/609250343/-1/NEWS0206>.

[40]Source: "Laundry Label Calling President an 'Idiot' is a Hit." Reuter's. 6 May 2004 <http://story.news.yahoo.com/news?tmpl=story &cid=573&c=7&u=/nm/odd_label_dc,>.

[41] Source: Judith Pinkerton Josephson, *Mother Jones: Fierce Fighter for Workers' Rights*, pp. 129-130.

[42] Source: Emily Keller, *Margaret Bourke-White: A Photographer's Life*, p. 76.

[43] Source: Michael Moore, *Downsize This!*, pp. 92ff.

[44] Source: James Barter, *Julius Caesar and Ancient Rome in World History*, pp. 58-59.

[45] Source: Bob Dole, *Great Presidential Wit*, pp. 32-33.

[46] Source: Donald J. Sobol, *Encyclopedia Brown's Book of Wacky Cars*, p. 62.

[47] Source: John Miller, editor, *Legends: Women Who Have Changed the World*, pp. 58-59.

[48] Source: Martin Hintz, *Farewell, John Barleycorn: Prohibition in the United States*, p. 64.

[49] Source: Cal and Rose Samra, editors, *More Holy Humor*, p. 67.

[50] Source: Angela Shelf Medearis, and Michael R. Medearis, *Dance*, pp. 10-13.

[51] Source: Walter Terry, *Frontiers of Dance: The Life of Martha Graham*, pp. 120-121.

[52] Source: Mary L. Davis, *Women Who Changed History: Five Famous Queens of Europe*, pp. 77-79.

[53] Source: Mark Oppenheimer, "For God, For Country: Remembering the radical chaplain William Sloane Coffin Jr." 14 April 2006 <http://www.slate.com/id/2139908/>.

[54] Source: Algis Ruksenas, *Is That You Laughing Comrade?*, p. 86.

[55] Source: Steve Jacobson, *Carrying Jackie's Torch*, pp. 124-125.

[56] Source: Michael D. Cole, *The* Titanic: *Disaster at Sea*, pp. 34, 37.

[57] Source: Val Halamandaris, editor and compiler, *Faces of Caring*, pp. 14-15, 18-19.

[58] Source: "Laconic phrase." Accessed on 29 November 2007 <http://en.wikipedia.org/wiki/Laconic_phrase>.

[59] Source: Kieran Doherty, *Congressional Medal of Honor Recipients*, pp. 42, 44.

[60] Source: Angele de T. Gingras, *From Bussing to Bugging*, p. 103.

[61] Source: H. Allen Smith, *Buskin' With H. Allen Smith*, p. 77.

[62] Source: David K. Fremon, *The Great Depression in American History*, p. 48.

[63] Source: Jim Brunelle, "Film shows how Howard Hughes trashed senator from Maine," 24 December 2004, *Portland Press Herald*.

[64] Source: Judith Pinkerton Josephson, *Allan Pinkerton: The Original Private Eye*, p. 41.

[65] Source: Diane Ravitch, ed. *The American Reader*, p. 223.

[66] Source: Sharon Salzberg, *Lovingkindness*, p. 43.

[67] Source: Virgilia Sapieha, Ruth Neely, and Mary Love Collins, *Eminent Women: Recipients of the National Achievement Award*, pp. 27-28.

[68] Source: Angele de T. Gingras, *From Bussing to Bugging*, p. 97.

[69] Source: Michael Thomas Ford, *The Voices of AIDS*, p. 210.

[70] Source: Eleanor H. Ayer, *In the Ghettos: Teens Who Survived the Ghettos of the Holocaust*, pp. 28-29.

[71] Source: Hyman Alpern, *Teachers are Funny*, p. 35.

[72] Source: Moira Davison Reynolds, *Women Champions of Human Rights*, p. 142.

[73] Source: Dick Van Dyke, *Those Funny Kids!*, pp. 67-68.

[74] Source: William R. Gerler, *Educator's Treasurer of Humor for All Occasions*, p. 201.

[75] Source: JoAnn Bren Guernsey, *Voices of Feminism: Past, Present, and Future*, pp. 47-48.

[76] Source: Morris N. Kertzer, *Tell Me, Rabbi*, pp. 171-172.

[77] Source: Tanaquil Le Clercq, *The Ballet Cook Book*, pp. 363-364.

[78] Source: Kathleen Tracy, *The Life and Times of Confucius*, p. 35.

[79] Source: David Bender, "Joie de Merv." The Huffington Post. 12 August 2007 <http://www.huffingtonpost.com/david-bender/joie-de-merv_b_60126.html>.

[80] Source: Richard Roeper, "Facing a draft, Nugent bravely wet his pants." 27 August 2007 <http://www.suntimes.com/news/roeper/529419,CST-NWS-roep27.article>.

[81] Source: John Kolasky, collector and compiler, *Look, Comrade—The People are Laughing ...*, p. 124.

[82] Source: a channel 4 newscast in Columbus, Ohio.

[83] Source: R.D. Wordsworth, compiler, *"Abe" Lincoln's Anecdotes and Stories*, p. 18.

[84] Source: Andrew Tobias, "LEGISLATIVE MANEUVERING." 8 October 2007 <http://www.andrewtobias.com/newcolumns/071008.html>.

[85] Source: Ellen Orleans, *Still Can't Keep a Straight Face*, pp. 20-21.

[86] Source: Lynne Yamaguchi Fletcher, *The First Gay Pope and Other Records*, p. 18.

[87] Source: Will Shank, "Doughnuts and name-calling." *The Advocate*. 8 December 2005 <http://www.advocate.com/exclusive_detail_ektid23241.asp>.

[88] Source: Zsa Zsa Gershick, *Gay Old Girls*, pp. 130-131.

[89] Source: Judith C. Galas, *Gay Rights*, pp. 47, 49.

[90] Source: Boze Hadleigh, *Hollywood Gays*, p. 347.

[91] Source: Lynne Yamaguchi Fletcher, *The First Gay Pope and Other Records*, p. 71.

[92] Source: Ellen Orleans, *Can't Keep a Straight Face*, p. 88.

[93] Source: National Archives in Washington, D.C.

[94] Source: Robert Lipsyte, *Assignment: Sports*, p. 98.

[95] Source: Daniel N. Rolph, *My Brother's Keeper*, p. 108.

[96] Source: Wanda Rutkowska, *Famous People in Anecdotes*, p. 45.

[97] Source: Susan Estrich, "My Hero." Creators Syndicate. 19 October 2007 <http://www.creators.com/opinion/susan-estrich/my-hero.html>.

[98] Source: Bettyanne Gray, *Manya's Story*, pp. 79-80.

[99] Source: John Spencer, *Workers for Humanity*, pp. 17, 22.

[100] Source: David K. Fremon, *The Holocaust Heroes*, pp. 50-51.

[101] Source: Linda Jacobs Altman, *Genocide: The Systematic Killing of a People*, pp. 31ff, 63.

[102] Source: Bud Greenspan, *100 Greatest Moments in Olympic History*, pp. 32-33.

[103] Source: Lawrence J. Epstein, *Mixed Nuts*, pp. 174-176.

[104] Source: Bill Adler, *Jewish Wit and Wisdom*, pp. 124-125.

[105] Source: Charles Anflick, *Resistance: Teen Partisans and Resisters Who Fought Nazi Tyranny*, pp. 49-51.

[106] Source: Linda Jacobs Altman, *Genocide: The Systematic Killing of a People*, pp. 52-53.

[107] Source: Debra McArthur, *Raoul Wallenberg: Rescuing Thousands from the Nazis' Grasp*, p. 119.

[108] Source: Eleanor H. Ayer, *In the Ghettos: Teens Who Survived the Ghettos of the Holocaust*, p. 10.

[109] Source: Judith Pinkerton Josephson, *Allan Pinkerton: The Original Private Eye*, p. 25.

[110] Source: Bill Adler, *Jewish Wit and Wisdom*, p. 103.

[111] Source: Stan Lee and George Mair, *Excelsior! The Amazing Life of Stan Lee*, p. 231.

[112] Source: Carlotta Hacker, *Humanitarians*, p. 35.

[113] Source: Moses Gaster, *The Exempla of the Rabbis*, p. 169.

[114] Source: Kathleen Tracy, *The Life and Times of Confucius*, p. 25.

[115] Source: Judith Edwards, *Lewis and Clark's Journey of Discovery in American History*, p. 80.

[116] Source: Angela Osborne, *Abigail Adams: Women's Rights Advocate*, p. 85.

[117] Source: D.J. Herda, *Thurgood Marshall: Civil Rights Champion*, pp. 90-91.

[118] Source: R.D. Wordsworth, compiler, *"Abe" Lincoln's Anecdotes and Stories*, p. 85.

[119] Source: Angela Osborne, *Abigail Adams: Women's Rights Advocate*, p. 68.

[120] Source: Philip K. Dick, *I Hope I Shall Arrive Soon*, p. 18.

[121] Source: Don L. Wulffson, *Amazing True Stories*, pp. 75-76.

[122] Source: Sir Rudolf Bing, *5000 Nights at the Opera*, pp. 123-124.

[123] Source: Roger Ebert, "Re: 'Glory,' 'Crash,' 'Geisha,' etc." *Chicago Sun-Times.* 22 January 2006 <http://rogerebert.suntimes.com/apps/pbcs.dll/section?category=ANSWERMAN>.

[124] Source: Stan Lee and George Mair, *Excelsior! The Amazing Life of Stan Lee*, p. 16.

[125] Source: Judith Edwards, *Lewis and Clark's Journey of Discovery in American History*, p. 101.

[126] Source: Ivar Bryce, *You Only Live Once*, pp. 11-12.

[127] Source: Michael Moore, *Downsize This!*, pp. 22ff.

[128] Source: a newspaper column by Jim Wright.

[129] Source: Carl R. Green and William R. Sanford, *Judge Roy Bean*, p. 33.

[130] Source: Rose B. and Nathra Nader, *It Happened in the Kitchen*, pp. 152, 160.

[131]Source: Don Hampton Biggers, *Buffalo Guns & Barbed Wire*, p. 158.

[132]Source: National Archives in Washington, D.C.

[133]Source: Gerald Fuller, *Stories for All Seasons*, p. 7.

[134]Source: Richard Fountain, compiler, *The Wit of the Wig*, p. 21.

[135] Source: E. Randall Floyd, *The Good, the Bad, and the Mad: Weird People in American History*, p. 70.

[136]Source: Phyllis Shindler, collector, *Raise Your Glasses*, p. 26.

[137]Source: Ron Chernow, *The Death of the Banker*, p. 22.

[138] Source: John Ferguson, compiler and translator, *The Wit of the Greeks and Romans*, p. 48.

[139]Source: Lewis C. Henry, *Humorous Anecdotes About Famous People*, p. 35.

[140]Source: Ellen Orleans, *Still Can't Keep a Straight Face*, p. 99.

[141]Source: David K. Fremon, *The Great Depression in American History*, pp. 21, 31-32, 36, 48.

[142]Source: Linda Jacob Altman, *Slavery and Abolition in American History*, p. 68.

[143]Source: Kae Cheatham, *Dennis Banks: Native American Activist*, p. 19.

[144]Source: Mary L. Davis, *Women Who Changed History: Five Famous Queens of Europe*, pp. 68-70.

[145] Source: Angela Shelf Medearis, and Michael R. Medearis, *Dance*, pp. 66-67.

[146]Source: Louis Michaels, *The Humor and Warmth of Pope John XXIII*, p. 44.

[147] Source: Carlotta Hacker, *Rebels*, pp. 33-35.

[148] Source: John Spencer, *Workers for Humanity*, pp. 48, 50. Actually, Dr. Bunche denied ever having said this, but it makes a good story anyway.

[149] Source: Yousuf Karsh, *Faces of Destiny: Portraits by Karsh*, pp. 40-41, 48-49, 140-141.

[150] Source: Chuck Close, "Capturing the Clinton charisma." *The Telegraph*. 6 October 2007 <http://www.telegraph.co.uk/arts/ main.jhtml;jsessionid=WVVLZYCQXXEYDQFIQMFSFFOAVCBQ0IV0?xml=/arts/ 2007/10/06/bachuck106.xml>.

[151]Source: Helen White Charles, collector and editor, *Quaker Chuckles*, pp. 99-100.

[152]Source: Joan Ryan, "A lifelong Republican's long winter." 24 November 2005 <http://sfgate.com/cgi-bin/article.cgi?f=/c/a/2005/11/24/ BAGBNFTM7H1.DTL&hw=Joan+Ryan&sn=002&sc=268>.

[153]Source: Tom Flynn and Karen Lound, *AIDS: Examining the Crisis*, pp. 55-58.

[154]Source: Jim Haskins and N.R. Mitgang, *Mr. Bojangles*, pp. 202-204.

[155]Source: Jean Darby, *Martin Luther King, Jr.*, pp. 64, 66.

[156] Source: Catherine Bernard, *Sojourner Truth: Abolitionist and Women's Rights Activist*, pp. 88-89.

[157] Source: Molly Ivins, "Remembering Ann Richards." 15 September 2006 <http://www.alternet.org/story/41688/>.

[158]Source: Doreen Gonzales, *AIDS: Ten Stories of Courage*, p. 94.

[159] Source: John and Kirsten Miller, *Legends 2*, p. 88.

[160] Source: D.J. Herda, *Thurgood Marshall: Civil Rights Champion*, p. 13.

[161]Source: Bernice Kanner, *The 100 Best TV Commercials*, pp. 18-19.

[162] Source: Steve Jacobson, *Carrying Jackie's Torch*, pp. 23-24.

[163] Source: Jean Darby, *Martin Luther King, Jr.*, pp. 11-12.

[164]Source: Bob Dole, *Great Political Wit*, p. 116.

[165]Source: Karen Alonso, Loving v. Virginia: *Interracial Marriage*, p. 93.

[166]Source: Kate Clinton, *What the L?*, p. 80.

[167]Source: Boze Hadleigh, *Hollywood Gays*, p. 59.

[168]Source: Stephen Currie, *We Have Marched Together: The Working Children's Crusade*, p. 77.

[169]Source: Bernard R. Brunsting, *Laugh!!! Your Health May Depend on It*, p. 80.

[170] Source: Dick Van Dyke, *Those Funny Kids!*, p. 107.

[171]Source: Wanda Rutkowska, *Famous People in Anecdotes*, p. 41.

[172] Source: Cal and Rose Samra, editors, *More Holy Humor*, p. 172.

[173] Source: Judith Pinkerton Josephson, *Mother Jones: Fierce Fighter for Workers' Rights*, pp. 10-12.

[174] Source: E. Randall Floyd, *The Good, the Bad, and the Mad: Weird People in American History*, pp. 48-50.

[175] Source: Moses Gaster, *The Exempla of the Rabbis*, p. 133.

[176] Source: Catherine Bernard, *Sojourner Truth: Abolitionist and Women's Rights Activist*, pp. 18-19.

[177] Source: James Barter, *Julius Caesar and Ancient Rome in World History*, pp. 80-81.

[178] Source: Don L. Wulffson, *Amazing True Stories*, pp. 80-81.

[179] Source: Carlotta Hacker, *Humanitarians*, p. 26.

[180] Source: John Miller, editor, *Legends: Women Who Have Changed the World*, pp. 108-109.

[181] Source: Donald J. Sobol, *Encyclopedia Brown's Book of Wacky Sports*, pp. 33-34.

[182] Source: Carl R. Green and William R. Sanford, *Judge Roy Bean*, pp. 23-24.

[183] Source: Donald J. Sobol, *Encyclopedia Brown's Book of Wacky Cars*, pp. 17-19.

[184] Source: Ron Chernow, *The Death of the Banker*, pp. 23, 105.

[185] Source: Bettyanne Gray, *Manya's Story*, pp. 26-27.

[186] Source: Ohio University Emeriti Association, compilers, *Ohio University Recollections for the Bicentennial Anniversary: 1804-2004*, p. 5.

[187] Source: Calvin Trillin, *About Alice*, p. 43.

[188] Source: Maureen Dowd, "A Cat Without Whiskers." 24 February 2007 <http://nevadathunder.com/?p=3574>. This article originally appeared in *The New York Times*.

[189] Source: Bob Dole, *Great Presidential Wit*, pp. 18-19.

[190] Source: Richard Fountain, compiler, *The Wit of the Wig*, pp. 15-16.

[191] Source: Nancy Shore, *Amelia Earhart*, p. 69.

[192] Source: Kathy Kiely, "Senator Takes on White House and Wins Fans; Robert Byrd's Bush-whacking Gets Cheers from Young Democrats." *USA Today*. 24 June 2003 <http://www.usatoday.com/usatonline/20030624/5268118s.htm>.

[193] Source: Alistair Cooke, *The Great and the Good*, pp. 270-271.

[194] Source: H. Allen Smith, *Lo, the Former Egyptian!*, p. 124.

[195]Source: Lewis C. Henry, *Humorous Anecdotes About Famous People*, p. 68.

[196] Source: Don Hampton Biggers, *Buffalo Guns & Barbed Wire*, pp. 210-211.

[197] Source: Noam Chomsky, "Imminent Crises: Threats and Opportunities." June 2007. *The Monthly Review*. Volume 59, Number 2. <http://www.monthlyreview.org/0607nc.htm>.

[198] Source: John F. Parker, *"If Elected, I Promise ...."*, p. 205.

[199]Source: Bob Dole, *Great Political Wit*, p. 21.

[200]Source: John Kolasky, collector and compiler, *Look, Comrade—The People are Laughing ...*, p. 49.

[201]Source: A column by Molly Ivins, published on Dec. 2, 2001.

[202] Source: Sir Rudolf Bing, *A Knight at the Opera*, p. 192.

[203] Source: Alain Chenevière, *Ramachandra in India*, pp. 5-6, 24.

[204]Source: Donald J. Sobol, *Encyclopedia Brown's Book of Wacky Sports*, p. 104.

[205]Source: David K. Fremon, *The Holocaust Heroes*, p. 70.

[206]Source: Stephen Addiss and G. Cameron Hurst III, *Samurai Painters*, p. 46.

[207] Source: Joseph V. Amodio, "Cate Blanchett returns as Queen Elizabeth I in 'The Golden Age.'" 9 October 2007 <http://www.popmatters.com/pm/news/article/49640/cate-blanchett-returns-as-queen-elizabeth-i-in-the-golden-age/>.

[208]Source: Benjamin Hoff, *The Tao of Pooh*, p. 148.

[209]Source: Michèle Brown and Ann O'Connor, *Hammer and Tongues*, p. 129.

[210]Source: Alistair Cooke, *The Great and the Good*, p. 159.

[211] Source: Erik Henrikson, "The *MAD* War on Bush." *The Portland Mercury*. Jul 12 - Jul 18, 2007 <http://www.portlandmercury.com/portland/Content?oid=365125&category=22148>.

[212]Source: Lawrence J. Epstein, *Mixed Nuts*, p. 231.

[213] Source: Gerald Nachman, *Seriously Funny*, p. 98.

[214]Source: Michèle Brown and Ann O'Connor, *Hammer and Tongues*, p. 150.

[215] Source: Joe Garner, *Made You Laugh*, p. 24.

[216]Source: Bill Hicks, *Love All the People*, p. xviii.

[217] Source: Martha E. Kendall, *Failure is Impossible! The History of American Women's Rights*, pp. 33-34.

[218]Source: Linda Jacob Altman, *Slavery and Abolition in American History*, p. 66.

[219] Source: Mac Davis, *Strange and Incredible Sports Happenings*, pp. 67-68.

[220] Source: Mike Towle, *I Remember Arthur Ashe*, p. 75.

[221]Source: Karen Alonso, Loving v. Virginia*: Interracial Marriage*, pp. 5-6, 24-25, 27ff, 45, 86.

[222] Source: Carmen Bredeson, *Ruth Bader Ginsburg: Supreme Court Justice*, pp. 10-11, 87-88.

[223]Source: Louis Michaels, *The Humor and Warmth of Pope John XXIII*, pp. 59-60.

[224]Source: Rev. Francis J. Garvey, *Favorite Humor of Famous Americans*, p. 5.

[225] Source: Gerald Fuller, *Stories for All Seasons*, pp. 27-28.

[226]Source: Rev. Francis J. Garvey, *Favorite Humor of Famous Americans*, p. 2.

[227]Source: Diane Ravitch, editor, *The American Reader*, p. 160.

[228] Source: Rose B. and Nathra Nader, *It Happened in the Kitchen*, p. 169.

[229]Source: Kieran Doherty, *Congressional Medal of Honor Recipients*, pp. 46ff.

[230] Source: Yousuf Karsh, *Karsh: A Sixty-Year Retrospective*, p. 49.

[231]Source: Judith C. Galas, *Gay Rights*, pp. 51, 54-55.

[232] Source: Beth Quinn, "Of phantom pain and cries in the night." *Times Herald-Record.* 28 May 2007 <http://www.recordonline.com/apps/pbcs.dll/article?AID=/20070528/NEWS/705280323/-1/NEWS0206>

[233] Source: Yousuf Karsh, *Faces of Destiny: Portraits by Karsh*, p. 142.

[234]Source: Thomas R.P. Dawson, *Amusing Sidelights on Japanese Occupation*, p. 43.

[235] Source: Alexa Dvorson, *The Hitler Youth: Marching Toward Madness*, pp. 34, 36.

[236]Source: Russell Johnson and Steve Cox, *Here on Gilligan's Isle*, p. 14.

[237]Source: Keith Elliot Greenberg, *An Armenian Family*, pp. 15-16.

[238] Source: Ted Widmer, "Arthur M. Schlesinger, 1917-2007." *The Phoenix.* 7 March 2007 <http://www.thephoenix.com/article_ektid35152.aspx>.

[239] Source: Debra McArthur, *Raoul Wallenberg: Rescuing Thousands from the Nazis' Grasp*, p. 115.

[240] Source: Joe Garner, *Made You Laugh*, p. 36.

[241] Source: Daniel N. Rolph, *My Brother's Keeper*, p. 39.

[242] Source: Tanaquil Le Clercq, *The Ballet Cook Book*, p. 33.

[243] Source: Sir Rudolf Bing, *5000 Nights at the Opera*, pp. 104-105.

[244] Source: Martha E. Kendall, *Failure is Impossible! The History of American Women's Rights*, pp. 29-30.

[245] Source: Carlotta Hacker, *Rebels*, pp. 39-41.

[246] Source: Emily Dugan, "Men only? You must be joking." *The Independent.* 16 October 2007 <http://news.independent.co.uk/uk/this_britain/article3063806.ece>.

[247] Source: Virgilia Sapieha, Ruth Neely, and Mary Love Collins, *Eminent Women: Recipients of the National Achievement Award*, pp. 151-154.

[248] Source: Helen White Charles, collector and editor, *Quaker Chuckles*, pp. 103-104.

[249] Source: Leslie Burger and Debra L. Rahm, *United Nations High Commissioner for Refugees: Making a Difference in Our World*, pp. 63-65.

[250] Source: Carmen Bredeson, *Ruth Bader Ginsburg: Supreme Court Justice*, p. 99.

www.ingramcontent.com/pod-product-compliance
Lightning Source LLC
Chambersburg PA
CBHW031426130726
47989CB00003B/1046